D0928195

THE
SECRET
SAUCE

THE

SECRET SAUCE

CREATING A WINNING CULTURE

KEVIN GRAHAM FORD
AND
JAMES P. OSTERHAUS

palgrave
macmillan

THE SECRET SAUCE

Copyright © The Armstrong Group, LLC, 2015.

First published in 2015 by
PALGRAVE MACMILLAN®
in the United States—a division of St. Martin's Press LLC,
175 Fifth Avenue, New York, NY 10010.

Where this book is distributed in the UK, Europe and the rest of the world,
this is by Palgrave Macmillan, a division of Macmillan Publishers Limited,
registered in England, company number 785998, of Houndmills,
Basingstoke, Hampshire RG21 6XS.

Palgrave Macmillan is the global academic imprint of the above companies
and has companies and representatives throughout the world.

Palgrave® and Macmillan® are registered trademarks in the United States,
the United Kingdom, Europe and other countries.

ISBN: 978–1–137–51288–8

Library of Congress Cataloging-in-Publication Data is available from the
Library of Congress.

A catalogue record of the book is available from the British Library.

Design by Newgen Knowledge Works (P) Ltd., Chennai, India.

First edition: October 2015

10 9 8 7 6 5 4 3 2 1

Printed in the United States of America.

CONTENTS

Foreword by Ken Blanchard   vii

Acknowledgments   ix

Prologue   xi

Section One: What Is Culture?

1 Holy Mole   3

2 A *Caliente* Company   19

3 It's Hot In Here!   35

4 If I'm the Problem, Then What?   53

Section Two: The Secret Sauce...Creating Culture

5 Getting It All Lined Up   79

6 When You've Lost Your Sauce   101

7 Letting It All Go   123

8 What's the Secret Sauce?   145

9 It Really Is All About You...Sort Of   167

Notes   187

Index   189

FOREWORD

One of the most encouraging trends in organizations in recent years has been the increasing awareness of the importance of culture. A healthy, people-centered culture is what makes an organization great—more than products, strategy, or innovation.

Culture matters. It touches how people are motivated and engaged, which has a direct connection to organizational profit and sustainability.

So how do you create a winning organizational culture? Through years of research and experience working with some of the world's top organizations, my friends Kevin Graham Ford and James Osterhaus have learned the answer to this question—and they share it in *The Secret Sauce*. With an entertaining narrative, real-world examples, and applicable lessons on nearly every page, Kevin and James show how to build and sustain a company culture where people have a sense of belonging, are fully engaged, and know they are contributing and making a difference.

I encourage you to read and apply *The Secret Sauce* to your organization—for the greater good.

KEN BLANCHARD
Best-selling coauthor of
The New One Minute Manager®
and *Leading at a Higher Level*

ACKNOWLEDGMENTS

We want to first thank our partners, employees, and friends at TAG Consulting. The principles in this book emerge from our collective thinking and client work as an organization.

We are also indebted to some dear friends and leaders who made time to talk with us. Thanks to Chip King, David Marsh, Tom Forney, Jeff Hussey, and Tod Bolsinger for taking the time to chat through their own leadership experiences.

Todd Hahn worked with us over the course of several years to prod, probe, write, and edit. It was truly a collaborative effort. And we have sincerely appreciated the support from Laurie Harting, our editor from Palgrave.

Our families have been incredibly patient as we have worked diligently for over three years to bring this book to life. In particular, our spouses, Caroline Ford and Marcy Osterhaus, have put up with a lot of frustration during the process of writing this book.

Finally, without our learning lab of client work, this book would be primarily theoretical. So we are thankful to have the privilege of serving clients in all three sectors: Public, Private, and Social. The process of writing this book has been, at its core, our own secret sauce.

PROLOGUE

It's been a long day at work and you don't feel like cooking dinner for the family. You're exhausted, the kids are under foot, hungry, and cranky, and your spouse says, "Let's just order pizza from Sal's."

With a sigh of relief, you glance at the frayed refrigerator magnet with the local pizza joint's delivery number and tap the digits into your cell phone.

Twenty minutes later, you and your family are enjoying a fresh pizza from a local business—no previously frozen ingredients from a national chain for your family! Sal's is run by a family of second-generation immigrants from Italy, by way of Brooklyn.

Everything is authentic, the service is fast, the prices are reasonable, and the pizza is delicious. The ingredients are fresh, to be sure. But the thing that makes Sal's "Sal's" is the amazing sauce! When pressed, Sal winks and smiles—"Ah, friend, I can't reveal the secret of the sauce!"

And it's all because of the sauce and the stellar service.

But it's not just pizza.

A loyal Chevrolet customer can spend $322,000 on Chevy cars over a lifetime.

A large company that buys commercial aircraft can spend billions of dollars over a period of just a few decades.

When it comes to pizza or commercial jets, customer loyalty can make a huge difference.

And it's not just for consumers. Employee loyalty is perhaps even more important than consumer loyalty.

Did you know that only 29 percent of the American workforce is actively engaged at work? And did you know that a full 17 percent are actively hostile toward their jobs and their employers? This means that over half of all employed Americans (54%, to be exact) are ambivalent at best about the place where they spend a substantial amount of their lives. The sad truth is that a majority of us could take or leave our jobs.

This has a very real—even stunning—impact on the bottom line and on the well-being and success of those of us who employ others.

One of the most influential business concepts of the last few decades is the Service-Profit Chain. The chain shows that there are linked relationships between profit, customer loyalty, value, employee satisfaction, and leadership.

Here's how it works:
-   Customer loyalty over time leads to growth and profit (think Sal's).
-   Customer loyalty is directly linked to customer satisfaction.
-   Customer satisfaction is based on the value of the goods and services that are offered and consumed.
-   Value is created by employees who are engaged, enthusiastic, loyal, and productive.
-   Engaged employees are linked to great systems and support at work.
-   Great systems and support come from a particular type of leadership.

Bottom line, profit and growth is not all about being smarter, more strategic, more ruthless, or having the best product, bar none. The finest strategies and the most highly educated workforces are helpful, but companies with these assets can lag and even fail.

The number one predictor of success is happy and engaged employees. And the way you get happy and engaged employees is through leaders who shape a certain type of culture.

In our work at TAG Consulting, we focus on all three sectors of work in American life—the Public, the Private, and the Social. It is vitally important to have engaged and passionate employees in each sector.

For instance, we work extensively with the Federal Aviation Administration, whose aim is to keep the flying public safe. We work with private companies whose objective is to maximize shareholder investment by sharing profits while serving the common good. And we work with not-for-profits in the Social sector that are committed to improving the lives of all in their communities—such as the church that seems to be "the place kids drag their parents to on Sunday."

The measure of success in each sector may look and feel different. However, every organization in each sector must have engaged employees if it is to live up to its aspirations.

Here's a quick side note for those of you who are not working in corporate America. While we use the term "engaged employees" here, the concept applies to volunteers as well. You'll notice that throughout the book, we'll use the terms "employees," "volunteers," "people," and "workers" interchangeably.

Each of us desires to belong, contribute, and make a difference. You'll find these principles embedded in a variety of disciplines—psychology, sociology, and theology, just to name a few.

In fact, we could argue that our greatest purpose in life is to be part of a creative community, as that is at the core of what it means to be human. We find creative communities in all three sectors in American society. Mind you, not all workplaces are "creative communities." Some can be destructive and toxic—to employees, customers, and even creativity itself. Many can be ruthless, serving the appetites of greedy and narcissistic leaders. Unfortunately, we even find this in some places that should be primarily about service and mission, such as churches and charitable nonprofits. But the workplace can be a place where we live as a creative community, a place where we can belong, contribute, and make a difference. Perhaps your highest calling in life is to discover your place and contribution within a creative community.

Regardless of the sector, people should be engaged in meaningful work that makes a difference.

One of our favorite authors is Charles Handy, a well-known business writer from England. We met with him at his home in England several years ago. Over lunch one day he explained what he had learned in business school—that a business exists to maximize medium-term earnings for its shareholders. He then spent the next two hours explaining how he had to *unlearn* what business school had taught him. In the end, he concluded that "a business does not exist to make a profit. Rather, a profit allows a business to exist to make a difference."

In our work across all three sectors, we have served organizations large and small—from storefront not-for-profits to Fortune 500 companies. We've been called into the highest levels of the federal government to work on projects that promise to change the very way of life of the American people. We've worked with social service organizations and churches that are on the front lines of human service. We've served commercial construction firms on the leading edge of industry-changing delivery platforms.

And what virtually every business school, consultant, or leadership author will tell you is this: what drives success—regardless of the organization's size, industry, or resources—is culture.

As so many management thinkers have said "Culture eats strategy for breakfast." Right?

Well, not really. It's not the secret sauce!

Let's be clear. Strategy is important. Operational effectiveness is critical. And culture does eat both of those for breakfast. Culture is a major ingredient. But it's not the secret sauce.

Confused?

Well, we have been too. But we have found that the very best organizations have discovered a secret sauce. Like Sal's pizzeria, they seem to have created their own "secret sauce," which leads to higher and higher levels of employee engagement and productivity, which leads to better and better value, which leads to more and more loyal customers, which leads to fantastic growth and profit. The secret sauce, in fact, results in a dynamic and engaging culture. Culture is a byproduct of the secret sauce!

We want to share with the process behind creating your own secret sauce that we have discovered—both through solid data as well as professional experience! It can be part of the success of your organization as well, and it will be unique to your organization.

It doesn't matter how long you have been a leader, how many employees or volunteers you have, how big your organization is, or whether or not you are flush or cash-strapped. The secret sauce is available to leaders of all stripes and organizations of all kinds. All it takes is imagination, passion, and the willingness to engage!

Let's start our discovery of the secret sauce on a beautiful golf course. And let's meet a flamboyant celebrity chef and a wise and somewhat mysterious golf pro...

SECTION ONE

WHAT IS CULTURE?

1
HOLY MOLE

If he could do nothing else, Gage Fabre could make an impressive entrance.

Gage slid into the circular driveway, popped his trunk, tossed the attendant his keys, and handed over a crisp $100 bill with a flourish. Gage started to sprint up the clubhouse stairs but something told him to pause and take it all in…the majestic mountain views, the immaculate landscaping, the air of quiet peace. It was all very different from the frantic restaurant kitchens, television studios, and busy airports where he spent most of his jam-packed life. Something about the place seemed to slow Gage down, a state of being he very rarely encountered.

Gage had grown up in the southwestern part of the United States, the son of a single mom who worked her way from waitress to the owner of a small restaurant that specialized in regional fare. Gage had basically grown up in a kitchen. In the early days, his mom had not made enough money waiting tables to pay for child care for Gage, so he had tagged along with her, becoming the restaurant's unofficial mascot, equally loved and shunned by coworkers and patrons alike.

Along the way he developed the personality that both protected him and set him apart from others—he was brash, hot-tempered, demanding, and ambitious. As a kid, he was impulsive, quick to change his mind, wanting what he wanted when he wanted it. But he was also fun and engaging, and lit up every room he walked into.

Yet he had a tendency to alienate people. He worried a lot about his image, and when anything happened that he feared would slight that, he would lash out, often with a tart tongue and at other times with a quick dismissal.

He loved the rough-and-tumble, the give-and-take of a restaurant—the need to improvise and overcome obstacles. He became a busboy, then a waiter, then a sous chef, and, by the time he was 16, was well versed in every aspect of running a business. When the kitchen got "in the weeds," he was at his best—seeing what needed to be done, alternately cajoling and encouraging his staff to do their best, to do things they had not anticipated they could do even as they resented him sometimes.

When he turned 20, his mom appointed him executive chef, and within 24 months the sleepy roadside joint had become a destination dining experience.

In a sense, the restaurant had been his family. His parents, who had met in the restaurant business, split up when Gage was not quite three years old. His mom had been the creative part of the duo, blending southwestern ingredients with French techniques. His dad, driven by greed and ambition, was currently in jail, his third stint.

Gage's only vague recollection of his dad was a fight, a lot of yelling, and a bottle of tequila, shattered on the kitchen counter. Gage remembers hiding under the kitchen table. He hadn't heard from his dad since.

His mom had lost everything then, but, with Gage's help, she was rebuilding the restaurant as well as a life. His dad had not been part of the picture from the time Gage was a toddler, and he had no siblings, so the kitchen was his living room and the other restaurant workers his brothers and sisters and cousins.

His "living room" became the place where he created and dreamed—where he learned to succeed and to fail, and how to bounce back from the failures. While he had to learn some of the management side of the business, he came alive in the kitchen. It was truly his passion.

And it was the place where he created his own sauce that was about to bring him riches. By most counts, he had already arrived. The locals all knew him, and he was establishing himself as a leader in his community. But second-tier fame and fortune wasn't enough for Gage.

Mole sauce is a crucial part of Mexican cuisine. Food experts guess that 99 percent of Mexicans have tried one of its versions. And there are many versions, all having in common the chili pepper as a base ingredient. The sauce is typically dark brown or red and served with roasted meat. It is delicious, earthy and spicy and warm, and often spiked with just a hint of chocolate.

Gage had made creating the perfect mole sauce his mission in life. And he had created a beauty—it was the star in his restaurant. Written up first in local media and later in publications such as Food and Wine and Gourmet, Gage leveraged his secret sauce (its exact recipe guarded like a state secret) into a chain of restaurants and appearances on the Food Network and the Cooking Channel.

Gage was hot-tempered, evidently like his father had been. And nobody triggered that temper more than his mom. With her homespun platitudes and old-fashioned values, she frequently cautioned him against fame and fortune. She told him that those things would destroy him. Gage knew enough of his father's story to understand that his mother blamed "ambition" for their split. Gage and his mom argued many times in her kitchen over months and years.

The drama rarely deviated from some predetermined script. After a few minutes of heated debate, things would cool off. His mother would put her hands by her side, shake off the anger, and calm down. Gage would lower his voice. And the aroma from whatever was on the stove would bring them back to reality. Then they would hug. The script never changed, but he was undeterred. He was driven to succeed. He didn't just want to win; he had to win.

His restaurant chain, aptly dubbed Holy Mole, had five carefully crafted locations, but he needed many more spots to satisfy his drive.

So far his success had allowed a very comfortable life, with room for him to indulge his love for Maseratis, lavish jewelry for his girlfriend, and to buy a McMansion for his mom in suburban Phoenix. But it wasn't enough.

Gage saw beyond the restaurant chain and the occasional appearances on the Food Network—to the creation of an empire. He envisioned a line of cookbooks, his own TV shows, and of course a lot more restaurants.

He was a young man in a hurry, already wealthy and relatively famous, fueled by his signature secret sauce and his passion and wanting much, much more. And it was that desire that had brought him here to this beautiful golf club today.

In two months, he would play in a celebrity golf tournament, alongside many of the most famous names in the food world. It was his chance to network and impress, to make connections that could lead to the next steps in the creation of his dreamed-about empire.

There was only one problem. Gage had never picked up a golf club in his life. Not given to half measures, he had asked around and been told the very finest golf teaching pro in the country was at Granger Mountain Country Club, nestled in the beautiful mountains of Banner Elk, a town in the western part of North Carolina.

Gage was here today to meet with the club's director of golf, Chip Long, to learn from the best so that he didn't embarrass himself in the tournament.

To do this, he knew he had to focus. And a phone conversation he had had in his car was making that focus difficult.

Larry Russell was the Holy Mole chain's executive in charge of expansion. Larry had a stellar background in franchising, and Gage believed he was just the guy to take the restaurant's 5 locations to 20. And then 100. And then 500.

On the drive to the golf club, Gage had been unspooling his vision for rapid expansion when Larry brought him up short.

"Listen, Gage, you know that no one likes rapid growth more than me, but there are some factors we need to pay attention to here. For one thing, we have to watch cash flow. For another, what has made Holy Mole so successful so far is that we have waited to open each location until we had done intensive market research and selected carefully vetted staff, all the way down to the busboys, because we know getting the right people in place so that they can succeed is how Holy Mole will succeed."

"Right now, Larry, the emphasis is speed. We gotta go with this momentum, grab this tiger by the tail. We want an empire, remember that."

Gage shook himself out of his reverie and looked around at the club's elegant yet simple interior. He glanced to his left to see a tall, thin, and fit-looking man in his mid-fifties striding toward him with a smile and an outstretched hand.

"You must be Gage. I'm Chip. Welcome to Granger Mountain."

The pro spoke with a confident but quiet voice. His smile was genuinely engaging and, interestingly, he gave off the air of someone who had all the time in the world.

Gage rarely had enough time to eat, unless he was tasting his latest creation in his restaurant kitchen. He couldn't imagine that this legendary teaching professional was anything less than slammed busy, so he decided to hurry things along.

"Hey, that's right! Gage Fabre. Great place you have here, coach. I love it. Thanks for making time for me. I got some new clubs—top-of-the-line Titleists, they tell me. The guy who fitted them told me that with my build, I'll be able to smack a driver 300 yards if I take lessons from you. Where do we go to start?"

Gage pumped Chip's hand enthusiastically as Chip just smiled calmly.

"I'm glad to meet you too, Gage. It is good to have you here to learn a little about golf and everything that is a part of this great game. You know where I would love to start?

How about a get-to-know you conversation over coffee or maybe some of our famous iced tea? We have all morning and, in my experience, the golf game starts with a shared beverage."

Gage blinked. In his hurry-up world, there was no time for shared beverages, get-to-know-you conversations, or leisurely pauses. How in the world was this going to help him look credible on the golf course?

But Gage had no time to protest. The tall golf pro in the perfectly pressed sweater and slacks was already heading down the large hall toward the club grill.

WHAT MAKES FOR A HEALTHY CULTURE?

We have said that culture is a key factor in organizational success and that the preoccupation of a leader should be creating and sustaining a healthy and vibrant culture. While culture is not the "secret sauce," it is a major factor, and we have to understand it before we can mix the ingredients that make the sauce taste so good.

Gage Fabre's genius was in fusing the southwestern ingredients of his childhood with French cooking techniques and Latin American culinary influences. Plenty of people use the same ingredients, and there are libraries of books and hundreds of YouTube videos whereby you can glean the basic French techniques. But the mystery comes when the Latin American influences enter the picture. That's where a run-of-the-mill mole sauce from a Mexican chain becomes something sublime.

Culture works like these influences—the often unseen yet all-important forces that make a pedestrian dish something worthy of being called a "secret sauce."

Here's our key question: if an effective leader develops and maintains a healthy culture, and a healthy culture helps lead to success, what exactly IS a healthy culture?

Walk into Nordstrom's, and you experience something. Immaculate surroundings, tasteful yet stylish clothing displayed perfectly, perhaps a skilled pianist playing at just the right volume to enhance the shopping experience while not drowning out conversation. And the conversation. Incredibly well-trained salespeople who seem to anticipate your every need and somehow manage to pick out the perfect shirt, tie, shoes, or accessory as if they have known you for years. Nordstrom's customer service is legendary, its environment is understated elegance, and its prices...well, pricey.

Walk into Costco, and you experience something else entirely. You feel as if you have stepped into an airplane hangar as you survey row after long row of plain shelves and fixtures bolted to the concrete floor.

There is a bewildering array of merchandise, from ice scrapers to industrial vacuum cleaners, to plastic vats of Jolly Rancher candy, to pots and pans, to a surprisingly intelligent wine selection. There are tons of associates around, and they are helpful if asked, but they will never stop to ask what you need—mostly they are scurrying around restocking the mammoth shelves and organizing pallets of bulk goods by way of beeping fork lifts.

There is no piano player at Costco, no understated elegance, nothing that Nordstrom has. But there is one big thing that Nordstrom does NOT have—amazingly low prices!

Nordstrom and Costco are both retail operations (they both sell clothes, as a matter of fact), but their cultures could not be more different. Nordstrom is all about fine goods presented by way of exemplary customer service in a soothing and classy environment. Costco is all about discount prices on middle-of-the-road goods presented in an industrial warehouse the size of several football fields.

Both companies are wildly successful, in spite of their very different cultures.

The cultural difference between these two well-known organizations is pallets versus personal service. Costco is proud that its culture is about being a high volume, low-priced warehouse where the customer basically serves herself. Nordstrom prides itself in catering to the customer's every whim. But behind the scenes, both companies go out of their way to take care of their employees, understanding that employee retention is critical to the bottom line.

You see, there is not one right or wrong organizational culture. The only questions are whether the culture you have is the right one for you, and whether it is a healthy culture.

Think about other organizations with distinctive cultures.

You get on a Southwest flight, and you sense fun and even love. You grab a burger and fries from Five Guys, and you get high-cholesterol goodness presented hot, simple, and fresh in a no-frills environment. You buy arugula at Whole Foods, and you are aware that you are purchasing the freshest and healthiest produce available outside of your local organic farmers market, displayed by associates with a knowledge of and passion for food. You order shoes online from Zappos.com, and you know that no matter if you love or fall out of love with the shoes, the company will wow you with their exchange policies and unrelenting effective and cheerful customer service.

It is easy to think that culture is a fluffy, soft aspect of organizational life—a "Have a nice day, now" lick and a prayer. In fact, culture is one of the most important determiners of lasting success.

The writer and blogger Shawn Parr defines culture this way: "a balanced blend of human psychology, attitudes, actions, and beliefs that combined create either pleasure or pain, serious momentum or miserable stagnation."[1] We like this definition because it is vivid and is drawn from experience. We have all known the stark reality of working in or with an organization where we feel stagnant and experience pain! Far better to come to work that is pleasurable and marked by momentum. Culture is the determining factor!

Strategy is key, pricing is important, marketing is crucial, to be sure. But culture eats all of these things for breakfast.

Parr points to the following benefits that come to any organization that has a healthy culture:

1. focus
2. motivation
3. connection
4. cohesion
5. spirit

Focus has to do with the organization being aligned around a compelling mission and purpose. Whether a large corporation, a small business, or a church, all organizations need a clear focus.

In 1999, we consulted at the highest levels of the United States Army. Their mission is a simple one—"To fight and win the nation's wars." Not a lot of fluff there. What this sort of crystalline focus does is to align the entire organization in lockstep with accomplishing mission and purpose. While we worked through hundreds of recommendations related to human resources, process improvement, and technology, pretty much every recommendation came back to this: does it help us fight and win the nation's wars?

In 2007, TAG began a strategic planning, or visioning, process with Mt. Pleasant Presbyterian Church near Charleston. This process allows an organization to establish not only who they are and what they value but where they see themselves going and how they plan to get there. Mt. Pleasant was one of those churches where membership looked good on your resume if you planned to run for local office. The church, initially founded in the 1600s, had the type of Low Country design that fit right in with the surrounding neighborhood. Golf after Sunday services was as common as shrimp and grits for dinner. But over the course of seven years, this "country club church" became a "missional church." How? Very simply by aligning around a clear mission: equipping our church family, engaging every member in ministry, following God's call into the world to transform Mt. Pleasant into a Christ-like community.

In 2010, we worked with Fairfax Hospital in Virginia. "The mission of Fairfax Hospital is to provide the highest quality of patient care in response to the behavioral health care needs of our community, by focusing on the experience of our patients and families." Our work focused on training within the human resources department, which helped focus employees on living out the mission on a daily basis.

In all three clients, we found that the culture was both created and supported by a very clear focus. Nurses need to know how to provide the highest quality of patient care. Soldiers need to know how every action feeds into fighting and winning wars. And church volunteers must have a sense of what it means to follow God's call into their own worlds.

Motivation has to do with why your organization does what it does. Buy a pair of shoes or eyeglasses from Toms and you get more than footwear and eyewear. Through its One for One program, every pair of shoes purchased is matched by a pair given to an economically challenged person in the developing world. And every pair of cool eyeglasses purchased guarantees clear vision or cataract surgery for someone who could not otherwise afford health care. The folks at Toms are about making a profit, and making and selling good product, no doubt. But their motivation transcends manufacturing, sales, and profit. Culture unleashes the power of motivation.

Motivation is external—tied to the mission. But it is also internal as well and is shaped in part by the environment.

One of our favorite companies we have interacted with has been Sturman Industries, with its gorgeous headquarters located at the intersection of Innovation Way and Sturman Parkway in Woodland Park, Colorado.

Situated on 450 acres at 8,500 feet elevation, with stunning views of Pike's Peak, Sturman's headquarters looks more like a magnificent mountain retreat than what it actually is—a center of high-tech digital design, producing products for some of the most powerful companies and high-level government agencies in the world.

Sturman is a technical powerhouse. Its founders have recently met with the head of the US Department of Energy, and it has added a former governor of Ohio to its executive team. But beyond the stunning success, what is striking is the motivating culture Sturman has created.

You get your first sense Sturman is different when you read their corporate mission statement: "Sturman is dedicated to making a positive difference in the world through our innovative products and company culture."

Stop reading after the phrase "innovative products" and you have a not-too-unusual corporate statement. But keep reading.

The commitment to "company culture" is on a par with the company's product, elevated to the same level of missional importance.

Just what is this culture? Your first hint comes with the corporate architecture. Exposed wood beams, huge windows offering soothing natural light and breathtaking mountain views, comfortable furniture…all of this extends past the showcase reception area to the inner sanctums few people save employees ever see.

It is a beautiful, restful, inspiring space—and it is available to each employee in the organization.

Sturman's leaders say that their culture and their environment are designed to "foster innovation, design, and creativity."

And there you have it. A technology firm that emphasizes that its employees are given the best possible environment in which to innovate and create, fueled by beauty and inspiration.

Can you imagine how motivating this is? To be offered a beautiful environment with no expenses spared to do important and influential work? Little wonder that Sturman is stunningly successful and its turnover is historically almost nonexistent.

Culture unleashes the power of motivation—externally and internally.

Connection brings together all parts of the organization, pulling people out of silos, connecting engineers to human resources, and soccer moms to coaches who worked their way up the athletic ladder. One of our clients is the division of commerce of one of the most storied Native American tribes. For many years, their new employee orientation featured a bus ride to some of the historical sites of the nation. New employees, whether or not they were members of the tribe, could see, smell, and experience the history of this proud people. Accountants shared bus seats with event planners, and human resource folks shared meals with maintenance workers. Years later, long-time employees remembered that bus trip and saw it as a unifying and empowering experience as they served the people of the tribe. Culture creates connection.

Finally, there is *Spirit*. In many ways, this is the least tangible of the benefits of culture, but it must not be ignored. Spirit is what brings life to an organization, the thing that animates it to be more than a series of soulless objectives or blanks on an org chart. From its earliest days, the founders of Southwest talked about associates loving each other and the flying public (when is the last time you experienced "love" in a bustling airport or a crowded airplane?). In more recent times, the founders of Toms built a nearly crusading spirit into their organization's DNA, with a willingness to forsake a measure of profit in order to serve people in need.

Take away the One for One program from Toms and you just have trendy shoes and eyewear. But One for One gives the organization a spark and a spirit that transcend the workaday world and brings passion to problems. Employee behavior and decision-making are shaped by a lively and passionate shared spirit.

Sturman Industries exemplifies spirit as well, even beyond its physical environment.

As we work with organizations, we are always looking for their code—the story that defines the essence and soul of that organization. You see the code of an organization as you study and consider as a whole its values, beliefs, norms, rituals, symbols, heroes, and architecture, setting, and décor.

You pick up on the code the second you walk in the door of an organization. It is reflected in the way the people talk, walk, dress, interact, and deal with customers and clients.

Go to McDonald's, and the code screams uniformity and consistency. Go to Chick-fil-A, and you will pick up on the importance of valuing each customer and demonstrating concrete acts of kindness and generosity. At Starbucks, the code reflects a hipster commitment to indie values and personal expression combined (a bit oddly) with a store-to-store predictability. Facebook's code is about breaking the rules and changing the way people interact in the details of life. Apple, in the words of founder Steve Jobs, has a code very much concerned with "making a dent in the universe" through its radical thinking and commitment to beautiful design.[2]

An organization's code answers questions about identity (who are we?), tradition (who are our heroes and how did we get here?), values (what do we believe in?), mission (why do we exist?), vision (where are we going?), strategy (how will we get there?), and style (how do we reflect our code?).

Remember how we described Sturman's physical environs? They are impressive in their own right, but their real importance lies in how they reflect the corporate code. We know this because we have seen the eyes of the founders, Eddie and Carol Sturman, light up when they discuss their physical plant. Here is what Carol told us:

"This building and these facilities were a one-time investment, and they appreciate in value. They are a fraction of the cost of salaries and other expenses. Yet most companies think only of cost-cutting when it comes to their physical plant…but we believe the environment we create reinforces the attitude we want—the positive energy, creativity, and teamwork that are vital to our success. We believe this beautiful environment communicates to our team that we value them and we want them to have a great work environment."

There is real spirit there, not just strategy. Valuing employees, fostering beauty and creativity even in a technologically driven industry, energy, teamwork—all are part of the gorgeous tapestry that is the code of Sturman Industries.

Eddie defines the essence of Sturman's purpose this way: "To make the world better through better products." It is a great statement, but hardly original. What gives the statement power at the corner of Innovation Way and Sturman Parkway is the fact that it is lived out and bolstered by an organizational code that is soulful and tuned to the human heart.

Culture generates spirit.

TAG'S DEFINITION OF CULTURE

Using our online employee engagement tool called The Engagement Dashboard, or TED for short, TAG Consulting has collected data from thousands of American workers from all three sectors in American organization life—public, private, and social.

After 15 years of gathering data, we believe that we have discovered the ingredients for the sort of thriving culture that gets us a step closer to the elusive but all-important secret sauce.

Culture is the realization of our desire to belong, contribute, and make a difference. In other words, a great culture is defined by three primary elements:

- high levels of employee engagement (the desire to contribute)
- a compelling organizational climate (the desire to belong)
- consistently effective leadership (the desire to make a difference)

These elements of a healthy culture are so important that each one deserves a separate chapter. That is where we are going next. But keep in mind, while culture is absolutely critical, it is not the secret sauce.

2
A *CALIENTE* COMPANY

Gage was hustling to keep up with Chip's lanky strides, when the teaching pro suddenly paused in the middle of a long hallway.

"Gage, would you mind if we made a quick detour to our pro shop on our way to the grill?" Chip asked. Gage agreed, and the duo reversed direction, made their way down a winding staircase, and entered a welcoming yet compact shop, stocked with balls and tees, gloves, and souvenirs available for purchase after a day on this world-famous course.

There was one employee serving a customer. Gage noticed that the employee—his nametag read "Bryce"—was out from behind the counter, very much engaged with the club member as they discussed the day's round and a schedule for golf lessons.

"Keep it up, Dr. Edwards," said Bryce. "You're making real improvement and it's clear that your investment in your game is paying off."

The member beamed, shook Bryce's hand, and exclaimed, "Good to see you, Chip!" as he left the shop.

Chip opened his hand toward Gage. "Bryce, let me introduce you to Mr. Fabre. He is one of our very important guests today." Bryce smiled at Gage. "Mr. Fabre, it's great to meet you. I have seen you on television! It's great that you are here at Granger and I hope you have a fantastic day." Gage nodded his greeting back, but glanced at his watch right after doing so. He was on a tight schedule and didn't have much time for detours.

Chip nodded at Bryce. "I'm glad I caught you as Dr. Edwards was leaving. I caught a glimpse of him on the practice tee and I've got to say his improvement was striking. His back swing is much more fluid and compact. You look to have done a great job with him."

Chip placed his hand gently on Gage's shoulder and steered him toward the door. "Bryce, I need to devote my full attention to Mr. Fabre, but I wanted to tell you one more thing. Make sure you wrap up today in time to get at least a little personal time in on the practice tee yourself." Bryce *smiled in response and waved goodbye to the two men. "Thanks, Chip. A pleasure to meet you, Mr. Fabre!"*

A few minutes later, Gage and Chip were seated in the comfortable bar area of the club grill, steaming cups of coffee in front of them. Gage was still a bit antsy to take his custom-fitted clubs to the practice range, but figured that with Chip's reputation he could give the man a few minutes to sip coffee and talk. Gage was a bit puzzled that such a busy and well-known golf pro was acting like he had all the time in the world, but he decided to surrender to the process, at least for now. He also had a question in mind.

"Hey, Chip, question for you. I read that top-flight golf pros, especially assistant pros, have to give up practicing their own game to teach others and run the operations of a golf course. There's just no time, especially when it's a famous course, right? How are you able to encourage Bryce to practice, especially when you guys are so busy?"

Chip took a sip of his coffee and contemplated the question for a moment.

"That's an interesting question, Gage. You know, in my years of doing this, I have learned something fascinating about the young men I mentor here in our pro shop. All of them are pretty darn good golfers, or else they would not be in this position. But for some of them, playing is more important than it is to others."

"Take Bryce, for example. A lot of his understanding of himself is connected to his skill as a player. He's competitive. He'll beat your brains out on the golf course. Even though he has more than a full-time job here, he still plays occasionally on the smaller regional tours, and does pretty well. In a way that doesn't make much sense. To make a living as a touring pro, you need not only skill but also endless hours of devotion to your craft. It's tough, if not impossible, to have a side job, especially one as demanding as teaching pro at a place like Granger.

"Bryce still has the fire in the belly, and I have to give him space for that. But in the meantime he is becoming—a wonderful teaching pro.

"Now take another young man in our pro shop, William. William is a wonderful player, but for most of his life he has wanted the life of a

teaching pro—spending all day at the same course, getting to know members, helping them improve their games. He's satisfied with all aspects of being a teaching pro, from the latest techniques, to extending hospitality to our members, even to course design and maintenance. I believe that young man is going to be a consummate teaching pro.

"What's interesting about William is that he doesn't feel the need to compete any longer. Bryce, in his free moments, wants to hit the practice range or compete in a local tournament. William wants to learn more about the business of golf. So, while I encourage Bryce to practice and play, I encourage William to spend a day here and there with other pros we respect and to go to workshops and seminars to expand his knowledge of what it takes to be a world-class teaching pro.

"What's wonderful to see is that Bryce and William support each other. William covers for Bryce when Bryce wants to play a couple of stops on the regional tours, and Bryce covers for William when William wants to fly to a seminar about running a better golf program. They have different personal emphases, but they both want the same thing—for the members' experience at Granger to be a pure joy and pleasure and an enhancement to their lives."

Chip checked to make sure that Gage had enough coffee and then changed the direction of the conversation. "But enough about the inner workings here at Granger. We're here to work with you, Gage. What brings you here today, other than wanting to get ready for a big charity tournament?"

Gage was a bit stumped by the question. "Well, I guess that's pretty much it. I've never played golf, but a lot of guys in the food world are real aficionados. If I am going to build the kind of business I want to build, to extend my personal brand and the brand of Holy Mole the way I need to, I've got to hit the links with these guys you see on TV all the time. I really want my own show, like these guys have. I'm as good as those guys are, at everything except golf. So, I've got to be good at golf. That's why I'm here."

Chip replied, "Let me ask you a question. Golf is in many ways both the most beautiful and challenging of games. It requires a lot of practice *and devotion and, to be honest, love. You've got to be able to practice 30 minutes or so several days a week and play at least once a month. In my experience, a golf game is not a means to an end, but an end in itself. Are you sure that it's worth that to you?"*

Gage was not even sure he understood the question. "Well, let me…" he began. "Look, here's the deal. I know there are a lot of people who treat golf as sort of a religion, who get all starry-eyed about it. And I mean no disrespect or anything, you have to know that. But I am a culinary artist and a business guy. Golf is kind of a means to an end. My passion is growing my business. I just need to be able to play a decent round of golf to help grow it!"

Chip thought a moment and nodded slowly. "OK, that's helpful to know what your passion is. So, what energizes you the most about your business?"

Gage leaned forward in his chair, warming to the topic. "It's the secret sauce, it's always the sauce. The sauce is the key to everything. As a matter of fact, I slipped a bottle or two into my golf bag for you and I'd be glad to comp a case to the country club chef too if you want!" He smiled, proud of his generosity.

"But, anyway, the sauce is a means to an end, but what an end. Here's the deal. Traditionally, food trends are about the main course—the protein, you know—beef or lamb or chicken or fish. If the protein is not the trendy thing at the moment, it's the cool, tasty, starchy side. Even vegetables have their run. But no one has built an empire yet on the thing that holds them all together…the sauce!"

Gage was gesticulating wildly now. "But it's more than just the bottled sauce with my face on the label. It's a whole brand, a whole lifestyle product line. People come to Holy Mole, they experience the taste, they cook with it at home, they watch me on TV taking it into new places and new cuisines, they share it with their friends on social media, it goes viral, it becomes a staple in their life. But I have to be in the right places and know the right people—so, voila, golf!"

Chip smiled serenely, got up without speaking, and poured coffee refills. He sat back down and thought for a moment.

"Sure, Gage, I can help you with golf, but I would love to ask you a few more questions. I am guessing that you developed your special mole sauce by yourself, with lots of time invested and lots of trial and error and love and late nights."

Gage nodded vigorously as Chip continued.

"So the development of your special sauce was a one-man operation. But to realize your dreams, you are going to have to involve a lot more people who may not initially share your love and passion. They may—they will—have separate loves and passions of their own. So, I would guess you are spending a lot of time trying to convince others to come along on your journey as you build your dream. Managers and accountants, and kitchen staff and waiters, and marketing people and television producers. Am I right?"

"You bet," Gage answered. "So many people just in the last couple of years. Sometimes it's a major headache to get them all on the same page, to get them to see what I see, to get them to care like I do."

Chip nodded. "I'm sure that's true, Gage. Let me ask you this. Oh, and you'll have to trust me, this has a direct bearing on your golf game as well. Three questions, actually."

"The first one is this: what do you want it to feel like to be your customer?"

Gage had never thought about it that way. "I guess I want them to feel like they are part of something caliente—hot as can be! I want them to feel like they are sharing a fun experience with friends and family, not just consuming calories. I want them to feel like a meal that involves my creations, especially my mole sauce, is a happening, not just dinner. I want them to laugh and tell jokes and make memories and come back for more. Oh, and I want them to tell all their friends so that I can keep my girlfriend, Sarah, in nice jewelry and myself in nice Maseratis!" he finished with a loud laugh.

"You have quite a vision, Gage," said Chip with a friendly laugh. "And I'll just bet that with your passion and energy you'll get there."

Seeing that both coffee cups were empty for the second time, Chip cleared the table. "Hey, let's walk outside, Gage—it's beautiful out there today!"

The two men strode out of the grill, back down the hallway and through the lobby, and onto the wide front porch with its breathtaking vista. Chip paused and breathed deeply, clearly savoring everything about the day and his surroundings. Gage wished he could share the bliss, but he was conscious of time's ticking and his cell phone vibrating repeatedly. "Let's get moving—empires don't build themselves," he thought.

After a few moments, Chip turned and looked Gage directly in the eye. "Here's my second question, Gage. And in some ways it is more important than the first one.

"It's this: What do you want it to feel like to work with and for you?"

Gage had considered what he wanted his customers to feel like before but, truth be told, he had never thought about his employees in the same way.

After a pause he replied, "Well, Chip, I guess I have to think about that. I guess I figured I was giving them the chance to be part of something bigger and better."

Chip just smiled the serene smile Gage was beginning to recognize. Out of the corner of his eye, Gage saw his Maserati pull up to the curb. The valet hopped out, dusted off the seat, and dashboard and waited expectantly.

"Gage," said Chip. "It has been a real pleasure to meet you today. I am mindful that you are very busy and we have filled every minute you have allotted. See you soon!"

Before he knew it, Gage was in his car and realizing two things. First, he had still not picked up a golf club. And second, Chip had not asked him the promised third question.

ARE YOUR EMPLOYEES ENGAGED?

Remember the basic premise of this book: in our multiyear study of organizations, we found that those with the strongest and best cultures could be counted on for operational stability and integrity. They were extraordinarily well-managed enterprises. And they had highly engaged employees, who have a God-designed desire to contribute, to belong, and to make a difference. We have found that organizations with high levels of employee engagement typically have these four characteristics:

1. Team members consider themselves to be empowered.
2. There is a culture of collegiality.
3. Management attracts top talent and rewards them accordingly.
4. Team members are fully engaged in their work and the mission of the organization.

EMPOWERMENT

"Empowerment" has become something of a buzzword in recent years. As such, it has gotten muddled as a concept.

Let's cut to the chase of how it actually shakes out day to day. Empowered employees feel valued, respected, and well equipped to do their jobs. They show up every day knowing they have the tools and training they need to do their work and that their ideas and concerns will be listened to.

Again and again, empowered employees say "yes" when we ask whether the following is true of their organization: "management does an excellent job of communicating expectations."

Several years ago, Starbucks realized that product quality was slipping a bit in terms of the process its baristas used from store to store. For a company based around creating a sensory experience and that takes pride in the utterly predictable high quality of its beverage offerings, this amounted to an existential crisis.

So, Starbucks went all out. It shut its stores down for a day to the public and focused on training and retraining its baristas.

But it did so with a twist. To be sure, the trainers emphasized standard methods of preparing the perfect cup of custom coffee or chai. But they also listened. The training day created a minor media sensation, and as baristas were interviewed they told reporters that training had not been done TO them as much as it had been done WITH them.

In other words, Starbucks asked its employees questions such as "How can we improve this process? What can we do to make the environment in our stores better for you as well as our customers? Is there anything we are missing—can you please coach us?"

In so doing, Starbucks emphasized mission and quality, while also empowering its front-line employees. They told their employees what they expected only after allowing those same employees a hand in shaping those expectations.

COLLEGIALITY

Healthy cultures feature members who are not only empowered but who also practice collegiality. Some people think that empowerment and autonomy are the same thing. They are not. Autonomy is total and complete independence. Empowerment is leveraging a person's individual strengths to achieve a common goal. Empowerment requires a shared direction, coaching, feedback, encouragement, and resources to accomplish the common goal.

Remember golf pro Chip Long's two assistant pros, Bryce and William? They wanted two different things out of their careers. Bryce wanted to be a teaching pro, but he still had ambitions to be a successful tour pro as well. William was sold out to being a teaching pro and being a subject matter expert when it came to running the golf operations at a first-class club.

Chip empowered his employees by discerning their strengths and creating opportunities for each assistant to leverage and maximize those strengths. But more than that he created an environment where each man supported the other.

Bryce covered for William when William attended a workshop or clinic on course or pro shop management, or when he wanted to shadow another excellent head pro. And William would work extra hours when Bryce wanted to compete in a mini-tour event.

In many settings, the two assistants would see their aims as mutually exclusive, perhaps even oppositional. *Why should I cover for him when he runs around chasing the impossible dream of being a touring pro? Why should I work extra hours so he can fly to some resort and pick the brain of a golf course superintendent?* Instead, the two young men saw themselves as colleagues. They trusted each other.

Like the healthy organizations where we have had the privilege of consulting, Bryce and William would say about one another, "my colleague's word is his or her bond." And this level of trust is a big part of what we mean when we talk about collegiality.

There are few things worse than feeling like you are always the last person to know something. One of the things that is worse is believing that when you try something new, you are on your own, left to succeed or fail all by yourself. Maybe the worst thing of all in the workplace is feeling as if you are not trusted and that you cannot trust—that you might well be uninformed or selectively informed about important things you need to know to do your job.

In a healthy organization, people can count on their colleagues. They are colleagues in fact, not just in name—they row together instead of competing with each other for resources, promotions, reputation, and face time.

A finance manager in a large corporation looked at us over a blueberry bagel and coffee during a break. "I know I shouldn't do this, but I call the accountants on my team 'my girls,'" she said. "It's because we all know we can trust each other, that we tell each other the truth, and that if one of us is struggling temporarily—having a bad day or something is going wrong at home—we'll cover for each other. Now, we demand performance of each other, we hold each other accountable. But we take this teamwork thing seriously, and we know our leaders do as well. I actually enjoy showing up every day and saying 'I am glad these are my colleagues.'"

RELIABLE MANAGEMENT THAT ATTRACTS
AND REWARDS TALENT

The late, great Peter Drucker was famous for saying, "Management is doing things right; leadership is doing the right things."[1]

What's interesting about this quote is that it is generally used to denigrate management and to point out the superiority of leadership, as if one can exist without the other. However, in the absence of skilled management, the strongest leadership will remain theoretical in nature and show a paucity of results. Management is more than important—it is vital. We have to do things right.

Why is this so important? For our purposes here, one reason stands out: truly talented people will not be drawn to poorly managed organizations. And no organization can be successful without talent.

Our research has shown that people are hungry to be managed well, even if they are already high performers. We've found three crucial elements to skilled management as it relates to attracting and retaining talent: just the right amount of supervision, timely and relevant feedback and coaching, and rewards commensurate with performance.

Managers who groom top talent know when to supervise and when to position themselves to offer help. The best managers are more like coaches than taskmasters, ensuring that their team members have all of the resources and support they need to do their jobs and that they understand the mission and objectives of the organization. After that, the best managers position themselves to make midstream adjustments and get on the balcony, taking a bird's-eye view of all of their team's activities.

In our research, one word came up again and again as productive team members described their managers—"helpful." There's a lot in that word. When someone is helpful, they provide the resources, advice, and counsel we need. We know they are available when we realize we could use help. But, once we are trained and aligned, they are reluctant to get in our way, much less micromanage.

The very best performers want everything they need to do their work so that they can shine, the support necessary to overcome internal and external obstacles, and the trust that their best efforts will be rewarded in both tangible and intangible ways.

Great employees are also looking for feedback that is consistent and helpful. They are looking for performance reviews, regardless of whether they are formal or informal, which are timely and actually linked to results rather than a seemingly arbitrary set of cut-and-paste objectives. And they expect to have input into the process and to be able to—in turn—evaluate those to whom they report. We hear the word "useful" repeatedly when strong performers describe their performance review process. They want to be managed in a way that is helpful and evaluated in a way that is actually useful in terms of day-to-day performance.

ENGAGEMENT

In an organization with a healthy climate, the end result is that employees fulfill their desire to be *engaged*. When they reflect on their jobs, they think things like this: "I matter around here. My strengths are being recognized and used around here. I am making a difference in and through my work."

In our employee survey, The Engagement Dashboard (TED), those organizations with a healthy culture consistently saw that their employees answered yes to questions such as "I get to use my talents and strengths every day at work."

Some organizations do this as a matter of course, putting employees through strengths-identifying instruments such as the DISC profile or the Clifton StrengthsFinder assessment. We recommend such tools and find that they can be extremely helpful.

However, we find that the very best organizations, whether or not they use the formal tools, end up identifying and developing managers and leaders who are talent scouts.

Scouting is important. A few years ago, the movie *Moneyball* dramatized the story of Billy Beane, the legendary general manager of the Oakland A's major league baseball team. The A's were a small market team, able to maintain a payroll only a fraction of that of deep-pocketed teams in major cities. Year after year, the A's lost their best young talent—the talent they had developed—to teams able to pay far more for the players' services.

In response, Beane developed a revolutionary approach to scouting. He looked at statistics and tendencies beyond the obvious, metrics other teams overlooked, to identify young players who could help his team win now. Since then, with few exceptions, the A's have been playoff contenders.

Beane's scouts knew what to look for because they had been schooled in a model of talent development that worked for the A's.

Do you know the kind of talent, the kind of strength sets that will help your organization succeed?

We're not talking about the obvious ones—smarts and experience and strong work ethic, though those are important.

We're not even talking primarily about some of the "softer" skills— teamwork and well-managed ego, and communication ability, though you don't want to ignore those either.

We're talking about taking a deep look at two things: "What does it take to win in our business?" and "How will we know a winner when we see him or her?"

If you can identify those people—fueled by your leaders' experience in the industry and the available strengths-identifying tools—and then deploy and encourage them, you will have made an important first step toward engaging your people.

So, having found them, how do you nurture such folks? The three ingredients for creating employee engagement are the following:

1. *Create a common language around strengths and skills.* Whether you use a ready-made program or create your own vocabulary, make sure that employees are talking to themselves internally and each other

externally about their strengths. We have developed strengths-based thinking and leadership in organizations of all types—from small not-for-profits to Fortune 500 companies—and we have found this common language and vocabulary to be indispensable.

In many of our client offices, employees will wear a small, colorful placard with their top five strengths around their necks after they come to a TAG workshop. Others will attach the placard to their briefcase or tape it to their computer case. We know we are making headway when we hear employees talk about their own strengths or say things like, "You know, Heather, she is really skilled at being adaptable—you want her to help manage change or navigate a crisis."

We recently led a pro bono workshop for a girls' high school volleyball team. At the end of the workshop, one girl walked up to us and said, "Thanks, I'm going to be an ER doc!" We weren't quite sure what to say.

Then she pointed out her top five strengths. "My number one talent is restoring things that are broken. My number two talent is empathizing with people in pain. My number three is problem solving. Number four is adapting to quickly changing situations. And my number five is finishing the task. That sounds like a perfect fit for an ER doc."

This 16-year-old girl may not be an ER doc when she grows up, but at least she has an uncanny sense of how to use her strengths.

2. *Make sure that managers are talking to employees about strengths.* So much manager-employee conversation focuses on simple tasks, the workaday "stuff" that must be done. Conversations that continue to circle back around to strengths are both more energizing and motivating and, as the service-profit chain shows, ultimately lead to greater success.

3. *Align your performance and incentive systems around strengths.* This is hard work because it requires that organizations put their people in places where the use of their strengths will help them to succeed, and this requires a great deal of intentionality. But once you have done

this work of leadership, an employee focusing on his or her strengths effectively will be able to trust that he or she will be promoted or rewarded—but most importantly—that he or she will be fulfilling his or her intentional design and desire to contribute, to belong, and to make a difference.

Engagement is vitally important in every organization. Businesses and government agencies need engaged employees. Churches and nonprofits need fully engaged volunteers and members.

But while engagement is beyond essential, it is not the secret sauce.

3

IT'S HOT IN HERE!

Gage was back in his office/test kitchen just south of San Francisco, bouncing through the small reception area that morning, shouting out greetings to his support staff, high-fiving his agent, making his way through the gleaming stainless steel kitchen to his brightly decorated office.

He sank back in his leather chair, propped his cowboy boot-clad feet on his desk and smiled at his agent, Mike, and Larry, his executive in charge of expansion.

"All right, fellas, what's up?"

The two men had requested the meeting. Larry cleared his throat a bit nervously and glanced at Mike, clearly deferring.

"Well, first, Gage, things are largely going well," Mike began.

"As you well know, things are trending in the right direction. Ratings are good, the restaurants for the most part are making money, the merchandise is selling better than we projected, cash flow is very, very positive, especially given the economic environment."

Gage slapped his desk in glee. "Awesome!" he roared. "That's what I want to hear! So what's so urgent I had to drop everything to meet with you guys right away? A new opportunity we can't pass up?"

Now it was Mike's turn to clear his throat and pause for a moment.

"Not exactly, Gage. You see, things are great on the outside but not so great on the inside. Normally, that's not my ball game—I am your agent, not your management consultant or executive coach. But people know you trust me, and people have been talking to me."

Gage knitted his eyebrows. "What's he talking about, Larry?"

Mike tilted his head in Larry's direction, and the executive nodded.

"We're doing great as a company and most everyone believes our greatest days are ahead of us. We're on the verge of expansion beyond our wildest dreams. There's only one problem."

The men had Gage's attention. "So, let's crush whatever that problem is, guys," he exclaimed.

The two men across Gage's desk were silent for a moment.

"There's no easy way to say this, Gage," said Mike. "So, I'll just say it. You're the problem."

Gage said nothing, just shot a steely glare at his agent.

Mike shifted uncomfortably, cleared his throat, but was undeterred. "I'll explain what I mean. Fact is, it might be better to say that this work environment is the problem. In general, people like you as a person, respect your craftsmanship, and believe in what we're doing here. But they don't like working here."

Gage shook his head, as if to clear cobwebs.

"You have got to be kidding me, man. None of what you just said makes one iota of sense. You just said people like me, respect the food, and believe in our mission. And I know I pay these folks well above industry standard."

Gage spread his arms out as if questioning the gods.

"So what the heck is not to like about working here?"

Larry leaned forward in his chair. "Let me take a shot at this from the perspective of an insider."

"It's not really you so much, Gage. Though you can be tough to handle. You're loud, which is fine. But you're also impulsive and quick to decide sometimes without having all of the facts. You yell a fair amount, sometimes even right after hugging someone. It can be exhausting to keep up with you.

"But, to be honest, all of that is OK. Most people know that you care about the company and in a general way about the people here. They also think of you as an artist, which I for one think is important to understanding you. But it's the other stuff that happens that has people on edge around here."

Gage was even more puzzled now.

"Guys, I'm missing it. You are describing personality quirks. Sure, I'm loud and emotional and impulsive and wear loud shirts and drive flashy

cars. Ninety-nine percent of that is me, and to be honest it doesn't hurt the brand. At heart I want people to love working here, to believe in the caliente principle, to get paid well and to have fun, like I do."

Mike nodded. "Gage, look, that's just the deal. No one is having any fun, man. To hear Larry and others tell it, it's all intensity, no fun to be here. People accept that they have to deal with your personality, work long hours, and be excellent at what they do. That's the price to pay for working in a no-holds-barred fast-growth environment. People get that. It's the other stuff... but here, Larry, help me out."

"Gage," Larry said. "You know how when it's hot in a room, you rush in and order the thermostat lowered? You can't stand it too hot, because the kitchen gets hot from the cooking, so you want it cold. You say you can't concentrate when it's too hot, can't get comfortable, you always yell, 'We gotta get the climate right, people!' Know what I mean?"

Gage nodded as though he understood and signaled Larry to continue.

"So, that's sort of symbolic of the whole experience of working here. The atmosphere isn't right, the climate isn't right. It's showing up in two main areas. The first is that people think you can't have a life and have a job here at the same time. People see the schedule you keep and the sacrifices you make and think there's no way to get ahead here unless they run the same pace. They feel an incredible pressure—like humidity in the air—to be here all the time, to be five minutes away at most to responding to an e-mail or text from you, to carry their phones poolside on vacation."

"That's tough enough. But people aren't comfortable while they're here, either. They never know when a surprise is going to hit, when someone is going to leave with no explanation. And they feel like their opinion is neither asked for nor listened to because you have everything figured out.

"This is tough to say, Gage, because you know I love you and believe in what we're doing here. But, look, the irony is that while you hate hot rooms, the fact is that the climate here is really chilly. There are some seriously good and talented folks who may not be around much longer because *they are not sure they can have a life or that they can trust the place, and all the money and success in the world can't make up for that."*

Gage felt like someone had punched him in the stomach. He responded by the book, expressing thanks to his agent and colleague, promising to think about what they had said, agreeing to read a white paper on work-life balance, agreeing to "do a better job of communication." Then he moved the meeting to a rapid close.

Inside his office, Gage slammed his fist on his desk in frustration. His first thought was to make sure the noncompete clauses were all current, especially with his top performers. He wasn't about to let the talent jump ship. But after a few moments, he calmed down and remembered how much money he had spent in legal fees the last time he sued a former employee. So he just sat and stared at the wall.

He didn't get it. In the restaurant industry, workers were typically paid little, worked like slaves, and were treated like interchangeable parts. For his part, he paid people well, offered generous benefits to full-timers, had every intention of awarding options when it was time to go public, and wanted everyone to feel like family, part of a caliente *family!*

It must be something else, he reasoned. He knew beyond a shadow of a doubt that his intentions were good. Yes, he demanded a lot. Yes, he made personnel decisions quickly. Sure, he could communicate his thinking more thoroughly. He supposed he could listen to input more. About some things. Not about the food, not really. Not about the branding, because he had a sixth sense about that stuff. And, yeah, not about the merchandise—he knew the kind of customer who was attracted to his brand and what they wanted better than anyone because he was that dude. But, yeah, sure, there must be some people with good suggestions about other stuff.

But he couldn't shake the thought that it might be nice to talk to calm, cool, collected Chip, or the "Zen golfer," as Gage had begun to refer to him with his buddies. The Gandalf guy who never asked him the third question. What was that all about, he wondered? And besides, he still needed to take some actual golf lessons! Gage picked up the phone…

CLIMATE IS KEY

In our consulting work over the years and in our research we have discovered that one of the most important components of culture is the Organizational Climate. This is rooted in our innate desire to belong to a creative community. We can learn a lot about a new client by walking through their work areas slowly, having casual conversations with people, paying attention to snippets of conversation during workshop breaks—in general, taking the temperature of the place.

In early 2014, Google made one of its biggest-ever acquisitions. It purchased a company called Nest, which makes a thermostat and a smoke alarm, for $3.2 billion.

Yep, Google—the worldwide leader in searching and in organizing information—bought a thermostat and a smoke detector for just north of three billion.

Many observers scratched their heads. What would a technology firm want with a company that makes boring commodities that hang on a wall in your house and are only noticed when they beep or you become uncomfortable? No one has ever looked at a thermostat or a smoke alarm and said "Cool!"

At least not very many people.

But the acquisition made sense. Nest makes thermostats and smoke alarms that are connected to the Internet, and thus can be used to gather data about customers and potential customers. Google's avowed mission is to "organize and simplify the world's information" and certainly house fires, carbon monoxide levels, and how warm people like their living areas are part of that data set.

But there may be something more at play here. Google realizes that climate matters, that temperature makes a difference, that whether or not a room is warm or cool has a big bearing on the happiness and productivity of the people in that room! The climate in your home makes a difference. The same is true in your organization.

Our research shows that Organizational Climate manifests itself in four key arenas:

1. interdependence
2. atmosphere
3. transitions
4. citizenship

How is the climate in your organization?

INTERDEPENDENCE

Whether or not you believe your organization functions as a whole or as a collection of separate parts has a profound influence on the way you lead, and as much as any other factor shapes your organization's culture.

An important part of being an effective leader is thinking in systems—looking at the forest, not just the individual trees. A leader knows that her organization is in fact a dynamic and complex whole, not just a collection of parts.

A beginning manager might look at her team and say something like this:

"Emily is great at solving problems. Jordan is terrible at solving problems, but he is great at smoothing the ruffled feathers of clients. Tyler is really good with all of that technical, IT stuff. And I am pretty good at making decisions. That's all I need to know about my team."

In fact, while those traits may be an accurate reflection of the talents of the team members, there are many more complex factors at work besides the cardboard competencies of the members of the team.

There are elements such as synergy—when the impact of two or more individuals is greater than the sum of the individuals; chemistry—the way different strengths and talents complement and enhance one another; rapport—the ability of team members to enjoy one another or at least to get along; and morale—the sense of optimism and confidence that feeds momentum.

Individual humans are complex, and so a collection of humans is very complex. The network of relationships within the system of your organization—whether it is 10 people or 10,000—is inherently complex. Any change in the group affects the group as a whole.

So a leader who is conscious of the reality of interdependence must learn to act in a new way.

Such a leader will focus on the relationships, the lines between individuals, more than the individual. When there is a problem within an organization, the easy thing to do is to identify a scapegoat for the problem. Get rid of Jim's bad attitude or Patricia's chronic tardiness, we reason, and our problems will go away. Then they don't, and we wonder why.

It's because there are relational, systemic dynamics at play. For some reason, Matthew feels it necessary to maintain a gruff, cynical exterior. For some other reason, Hannah is so anxious about going to work that she can never bring herself to be on time. Perhaps Matthew's interactions with Michael fuel his insecurities, and perhaps Taylor terrifies Hannah with her relentless demands, which are in turn fueled by the way Ben makes Taylor feel that she never measures up.

The answers to chronic problems in the organization are rarely, if ever, safely laid at the feet of any one person. The wise leader will see past personalities and focus on the way individuals within the group relate to one another.

In organizations with healthy interdependence, members say things like these responses from our survey, The Engagement Dashboard (TED):

- When a problem repeats itself, I understand that I may be part of the problem.
- My actions are influenced by those around me, even though I am ultimately responsible.

– In turn, my actions influence those around me.

– The way people interact with each other takes on a
  predictable pattern over time and that offers real insight
  into the way things work around here.

ATMOSPHERE

When the city of Charlotte received its first NBA professional basketball team, it was called the Hornets, and as of the end of 2014 the
team was renamed the Hornets even though it was not the same team
and even though the New Orleans team used to be called the Hornets…but that's not important right now.

On opening night of the team's first season, a local college's cheer-
leading team entertained Hornets fans with this chant: "It's hot in here!
It's hot in here! There must be a Hornet in the atmosphere!"

Catchy, right? The point was that the advent of the team meant
that things were different now in Charlotte. Long an up-and-coming
city, Charlotte had reached the big time, at least in terms of professional sports. The very air was different! The atmosphere had changed.
There was a buzz, and it wasn't just the Hornets! The whole city had
changed.

Every organization has a prevailing atmosphere as well. You can
sense it in the response of employees to two words: comfort and fun.

Employees in organizations with a healthy atmosphere as part
of their culture feel comfortable with the differences that are part of
the modern workplace. Differences can be obvious—gender or eth-
nic. But they can also be subtle—differences in temperaments, talents, and strengths. These employees are comfortable in trusting that
the organization cares as much about its people as it does its profit
and that there are policies in place that support family and personal
time.

And employees in organizations with the very best atmospheres
tell us again and again that they believe that working where they do

is good for their health and that it is a FUN place to make a living in support of making a life.

Red Ventures, located in South Carolina, is consistently ranked at or near the top of "best places to work" in its area. It is one of the fastest-growing companies in its region, to be sure, but its real differentiator is its freewheeling and fun culture. Here is an example from the company's website (www.redventures.com) where the company describes what an employee can expect to experience:

Who wouldn't want to work at a place like that, right?

The fact is that Red Ventures demands a lot of its team, and new team members are often required to work shifts that many people find undesirable. They are in a tough, highly competitive business with a lot of pressure.

In the face of this, Red Ventures' leaders have determined to make their atmosphere one marked by caring for employees, providing perks and privileges, and creating fun. If fun could be measured by a thermostat, the temperature at Red Ventures is just right!

But there's more than fun and games. Note the emphases on advanced technology (the right tools for the job), the chance to present ideas (my voice is heard here), and on being motivated by the people around you (a recognition that the organization is a system characterized by interdependence). All of these factors shape the quality of the organization's climate.

TRANSITIONS

Transitions are hard, and the American economy has experienced more than its fair share in the last few years. People move on and organizations have outgrown other people. There are the inevitable contractions connected with recession, mergers and acquisitions, and competitive struggles. Everyone expects transition.

But how an organization handles transition can make or break it in terms of climate and culture.

Transitions do not just happen when someone is let go or moves on. There are three major times for transition:

1. when a team member enters the organization
2. as a team member progresses within the organization
3. when a team member leaves the organization

When someone enters an organization, they begin to sense the culture from day one—actually, they pick it up in the hiring process. Starting a new job is both tough and exciting all at once. Exciting because of new possibilities. Tough because it may involve leaving old friendships and partnerships and navigating a whole new environment. The organizations with the healthiest cultures pay attention to these all-important moments.

Newcomers receive effective training and organization. They find opportunities to be mentored and to "learn the ropes." There is someone to explain "how things really get done around here." They are made to feel welcome and understood even when they do not understand very much.

A distinguishing mark of organizations with healthy climates is that its leaders are intentional about these things. There will always be someone to tell the newcomer "how things really work here," but intentionality determines whether the message is a cynical, world-weary one or one fresh with hope and infused with the organization's core values.

Smart leaders recognize that the newcomer phase is important for creating engagement, attraction and loyalty, for all the right reasons.

As time goes on, transition continues to be a factor. Newcomers become old hands, look around them and see whether the team is retaining valuable employees or not, whether promotions are fairly rewarded or are a product of the politics of the good old boys/girls network, and whether team members are listened to, ignored, or condescended to.

The healthiest climates honor informal leadership as well as formal leadership. Sure, there are titles, dashes and lines on an org chart, and accountabilities…but there is also a sense that the best ideas can come from unexpected places and that a leader does not need to be an "executive," "manager" or "partner" to play a key role in the direction of the organization.

Finally, when people leave—voluntarily or involuntarily—this wrenching transition is handled with grace and skill in organizations with healthy atmospheres. Changes rarely surprise people, because a premium has been placed on communication. People are encouraged to discuss their opinions and points of view on change, and those who leave are honored as they go, even if the reason for their leaving was difficult.

Transitions of all kinds are navigated well when you use these three practices:

1. Credibility—leaders are even-handed and fair, and so make deposits of trust, which can be borrowed against when tough changes have to be instituted.
2. Transparency—unless trade secrets that would compromise competitive advantage are at stake, leaders default to sharing details about the conditions that shape transition decisions, the rationale for unpopular decisions, and the long-term effects on all those in the organization.
3. Honor—in the case of terminations and layoffs, unless an employee was dismissed for ethical or legal reasons every effort is made to honor those leaving, thanking them for their contributions and pointing out their positive characteristics. This is the right thing to do for the one leaving, and it engenders trust and loyalty among those staying!

CITIZENSHIP

Pura Vida sells great coffee, cool coffee-related products, and stylish break room supplies, and even does a great job of supplying coffee kiosks for not-for-profits with walk-through traffic. But that does not begin to scratch the surface of the mission of Pura Vida. Good never tasted so good. Buy Coffee. Create Good.

Spanish for "pure life" and the virtual national motto of Costa Rica, Pura Vida speaks of clean air, fresh water, and a healthy, relaxed, fun-filled lifestyle. But that lifestyle is historically unavailable to coffee farmers in the developing world, many of whom work, live, and raise families in unsafe conditions for very little compensation.

So, Pura Vida sells only Fair Trade and organic-certified coffee, insuring that a portion of the profits go to farmers and that they can live and work in a clean environment. This is a very good thing—laudable even—but Pura Vida is not the only company to do so.

Our friend, majority owner Jeff Hussey, talks about the real motivation behind Pura Vida: "A lot of it is about solving the world's clean water problem."

Wow, that is a mouthful, and not just a mouthful of premium java!

It is what some would argue is the world's leading economic and public health issue—access to clean water for drinking, bathing, cooking. It is a huge problem. Combine this with Pura Vida's commitment to providing just returns for hard-working coffee farmers and their communities, and you seem to have the recipe for a UN-style not-for-profit organization. But Pura Vida is very much about making a profit.

How in the world do you bring the do-good motive and the profit motive together?

The answer speaks to Pura Vida's Organizational Climate and its commitment to citizenship.

And it is summed up in their clever motto: "It's better to give than to receive. Unless you can do both!"

This is a company that invests profits into water filtration for villages in Guatemala, economic development for poverty-stricken towns in Mexico, and clean water and sanitation in Guatemala.

It accomplishes much of this through a strategic partnership with a public charity called the Create Good Foundation, which exists to aid coffee-growing communities throughout the world through, in part, digging latrines, building wells, and bringing water filtration to households.

Making pure and healthy water available is a monumental challenge in our world.

Pura Vida makes no bones about it. Their goal is to solve the world's water problem one family and one village at a time. But its approach is more than meets the eye. In addition to clean water, a major issue in these communities is the lack of an economic infrastructure to provide jobs and hope. Pura Vida and its partners invest in the technical aspects of water filtration and well digging, but they are also involved in projects and investments that create small micro-businesses that employ workers and lift families out of abject poverty.

What is notable about Pura Vida is that this is not just part of what they do, like a United Way drive or a Habitat for Humanity employee volunteer day (as helpful as those may be). For Pura Vida, their mission is woven into the very fabric of their existence. It is the leading edge of their strategy and hence shapes their culture. Citizenship is not an optional add-on or a source of corporate tax deductions—it is part and parcel of why Pura Vida exists.

Pour a nice, Fair Trade-certified cup of coffee and take a look at their web page—www.puravidacreategood.com. It is hard to tell what comes first: the mission or the coffee. Now *study* the webpage. It is clear that BOTH are critical. The company is deeply committed to selling great-tasting premium coffee and cool coffee-related gear. But behind that commitment is a mission—"the farmer comes first."

Here is how Jeff describes his quest to us. "To begin, faith has been the primary motivator behind all of my philanthropic efforts. Long before I achieved any substantive financial success, I committed to give 20 percent of my earnings to God. I did so by forming a foundation and contributing a fifth of my stock to it. As the value of the foundation began to rise, I became increasingly aware of the manifold challenges there are to effective philanthropy. I discovered that despite their good intentions, some charitable organizations do as much to perpetuate certain problems as they do to solve them. Determined to avoid similar outcomes, I recognized the need for a different approach, a more direct, businesslike approach that I could be involved in personally.

"The results of my philanthropic efforts up to that point had convinced me that the problems of the poor in the developing world will be solved by business, not charity. My desire for personal involvement ruled out far-away or hard places to reach such as Africa or Haiti. So I started to focus on Guatemala, a country with a lot of people and a lot of problems. As water is a universal need and nearly every water source in Guatemala is polluted, an opportunity to make a difference existed. I could assume that people had access to water, but that water may not be safe to drink. Those observations and the at times not so gentle call of God led me to the business (and charity) of point-of-use water filtration.

"It is so encouraging to me to see what a difference a $30 filter can make to a family in a very short time: 1) their overall health improves because they consume more clean safe water and eliminate waterborne pathogen-related illness; 2) they spend less time and money gathering or buying firewood to boil water; 3) money that would otherwise go to purchase firewood can instead be spent on food, further improving health. And the list goes on."

If you ever have the chance, talk to one of their employees or to Jeff Hussey. The office walls are unpainted—they'll get around to it one day, but right now it just does not seem that important. One executive told www.seattlepi.com, "It's very motivating to know that everything we do at Pura Vida is centered around our mission to create good."[1]

Now, reflect on this. "Create Good" is even in their website's URL!

Everything—*everything*—at Pura Vida is imbued with this sense of a commitment to citizenship.

Not every organization will hold its corporate mission to do good as front and center, but every organization can be a great citizen—of their community and of the world. This is the right thing to do AND it is good business, because employees get more deeply engaged when they believe deeply that their work is about something bigger than just their work. As we have said repeatedly, we have an innate desire to belong, contribute, and make a difference. Part of a great culture is being a great citizen. And citizenship is vital to creating a great climate.

And while organizational climate is another key to success...it is still not the secret sauce.

4

IF I'M THE PROBLEM, THEN WHAT?

Gage was back in the North Carolina mountains, meeting with Chip. Before, he had been eager to get on the golf course, or at least the practice range. Now, he was eager to talk with the pro.

Over another cup of coffee in the grill room, Gage detailed the tough conversation he had had with Mike and Larry where the two men had told him, reluctantly, that he was the problem with the organization. In spite of its growth and potential, the men had reported, the employees were demoralized and tentative, unsure of what they were going to get on any given day.

In a follow-up conversation, Larry had said, "Gage, everyone here believes in your talent and in your vision. Everyone knows that at the end of the day you are a really good guy. The only question people have is if they can count on you to come through in the end for them and for the company, or if you will be off on some sort of tangent."

It was that last comment that had driven Gage to request another meeting with Chip and fly across the country again.

Gage blew the surface of his steaming coffee. "I always thought that being a visionary was my great strength. Of course, other than being a great chef. But I'm ambitious. I won't settle for mediocrity. I want the best out of my company and out of my employees. There are no barriers to growth that I can't overcome. I assumed that my vision made for an exciting atmosphere to work in. Now, my manager and agent are telling me my strength is my weakness? I just don't get it."

Chip thought for a long time.

"Gage, there is no doubt you are a visionary leader. You have built a very strong brand, known nationally, in a field that is as creative as it is competitive. It's good to get the feedback that your employees appreciate your acumen and vision."

Chip paused before continuing.

"But I wonder if you are actually being effective as a leader."

The last time Gage and Chip had met, Gage knew, he would have exploded at such a comment.

But something felt different this time around. The conversation with Larry and Mike had taken him aback, and there was something about Chip's demeanor that made even the hardest of questions easier to stomach. They didn't feel like accusations.

Gage's reply was cautious. "I guess I would need to know what you mean by effective."

"You've done a lot of things right in your business. You have good ideas, lots of energy, creativity, and have been willing to take risks. You've learned how to create and grow a brand. And, maybe best of all, you have hired smart business people to run the day-to-day operations for you."

"I think that last factor has meant that your business has been largely efficient up till now. But efficiency is very different from effectiveness.

"Every organization will rise and fall based on the effectiveness of its top leader, especially when that leader is also a founder. Your ideas and energy and the efficiency of your managers can only take you so far.

"Based on what you are telling me, Gage, I am wondering if your people think of you as dependable. Brilliant, yes. Kindhearted, certainly. Creative, without a doubt.

"But being dependable is something else entirely.

"As your organization matures and grows and the workforce expands, it is going to be critical for you to make sure that your folks feel like they can count on both the organization and on you. That they can depend on both."

Gage was intrigued. "Tell me more about what you mean…"

"In an uncertain world and economy, people, more than ever, are look-ing for dependability and security. People need trust. That doesn't mean

leaders have to be parents, but it means they have to recognize this reality and adapt accordingly.

"But, truth be told, it doesn't matter what the economic climate is. People need to know they can count on their leaders to come through in certain ways. People often learn this kind of dependability from their role models—their parents, their bosses, their coaches. Dependability doesn't come naturally, but it can be learned.

"Gage, I would love for us to talk about golf some today, but I feel compelled to ask you a question. Remember a while back, I said I had three questions? Well here's the third one...

"Who do you need to be to insure that your people can depend on you, that they can trust you as their leader? After all, if you are going to leverage your innate desire to belong, contribute, and make a difference, you have to be effective. And the only way to truly be effective is to be trustworthy.

"I'm not sure people know you, Gage. Sure, they know that you're a visionary and that you've built a great brand. But to trust you, they have to know what you're really all about. I'm not asking what you need to do, Gage. I'm asking who you need to be. There's a big difference."

Gage sat over his coffee, not sure how to respond. Then, he nervously chuckled, "Okay, doc, I'll think about it. But are we ever going to work on my swing?"

Chip sighed. Evidently, Gage wasn't quite ready for that question. As he walked out of the room, he turned to Gage and said "Get your clubs and meet me on the range in five minutes."

TRUST AND LEADERSHIP EFFECTIVENESS

"As you can see, the underlying fundamentals of our businesses are very strong—indeed the strongest they've ever been. But regrettably, that's not what Wall Street is focusing on, and I doubt that's what you're focusing on. This inquiry will take a lot of time on the part of our accountants and lawyers and others, but it will finally put these issues to rest.... Despite the rumors, despite the speculation, the company is doing well, both financially and operationally."

These comments came from Ken Lay on October 22, 2001, during a speech given to several employees of the Enron Corporation.

At the time, Lay was the Chairman and CEO of Enron—a multibillion-dollar corporation that had been named "America's Most Innovative Company" by *Fortune* magazine for six consecutive years. At the time, Lay and executives like Jeffrey Skilling and Andrew Fastow were respected, powerful, and wealthy beyond imagining. And at the time, Enron's thousands of employees and shareholders still had hope that the warning signs and whispered rumors would all turn out to be nothing more than a misunderstanding.

But on December 2, just a few weeks later, Enron filed for the largest Chapter 11 bankruptcy in the history of the United States.

After finishing his speech on October 22, Lay indulged in a brief Q & A session with the Enron employees in the room. As luck would have it, the first question presented to him was both hilarious and stunningly prophetic. "I would like to know if you are on crack," said Lay, reading the question out loud. "If so, that would explain a lot. If not, you may want to start, because it's going to be a long time before we trust you again."[1]

Trust. That is the operative word, both for this chapter and, to some extent, for this entire book.

Our study of organizational culture revealed that leadership effectiveness is a crucial component of both employee engagement and a thriving organization. And there is one word that encapsulates leadership effectiveness. You guessed it. Trust.

The Engagement Dashboard includes 98 questions that employees rate on a 1 to 5 scale. We have had thousands of American workers take the survey. Each organization is compared, using percentiles, to our national database.

With all this data, we were astounded to learn that one question stood head and shoulders above all the others. All of the questions had a strong correlation to this one question. If we scratched the other 97 questions, we could probably predict the long-term success or failure of the organization based on this question.

Management can be counted on to come through when needed.

That's dependability in a nutshell. It all boils down to that one concept. Can leadership be trusted?

Chase had secured a year-long internship at a well-respected company right after graduating from college. The company had a reputation for taking good care of its people, supporting the development of its workforce, and being a "plus sign" on any resume. The internship program was considered a crown jewel of the company.

Chase was from a working-class family, had significant college debt, and the internship did not pay much. But he knew he had to scrape together what money he could to get from the East Coast to the West Coast, where the company was based. It could be the chance of a lifetime, or at least of a career.

He got off to a great start at the company, enjoyed the work, and developed a trusting relationship with the executive assigned to be his mentor.

Then one Tuesday afternoon, just three months into his internship, Chase received a life-changing call.

His father had suffered a serious heart attack, and the doctors were not sure whether he would live. Chase desperately wanted to go home, his mom needed him to come home, but there was simply no way to cobble together the funds.

Heartbroken and nearly desperate, Chase explained the situation to his supervisor and asked if he could have the rest of the afternoon off. The supervisor quickly agreed, and Chase went for a walk in a nearby park to walk off his anxiety and try to come up with a plan to get home. But no plan came.

Several hours later, Chase's phone rang. It was the executive from the company assigned to be Chase's mentor. The man expressed his condolences and concern and made an amazing offer.

"Chase, I know money is tight for you and your family. I also know that you need to get home to be with your folks. As you know, I travel a lot and I have a lot of frequent-flyer points. I've taken the liberty of booking a flight home for you, leaving tomorrow morning. And, of course, you must stay as long as you need to. Your internship will be here for you when you return."

Chase was stunned and could barely speak, but his mentor continued.

"One more thing. Our CEO's brother is perhaps the most respected cardiologist in your hometown. Our CEO called him and asked him if he would be willing to check into your dad's case personally. He agreed and is moving on that now."

Needless to say, Chase never forgot the gesture of care and concern.

Going to these lengths rather than just expressing sympathy indicated a profound level of dependability on the part of that company's leaders, a trait that was a defining part of the organization's culture.

There is everyday, garden-variety dependability, the irreducible minimum an organization must provide to cover the basics. Do team members need to know that leaders will provide clear direction, provide the resources necessary to do the job, and keep their word? Sure. Must volunteers know that their leaders will advocate for them when need be and go to bat to get the team the resources and opportunities it needs? Absolutely. But that's the bare minimum.

Organizations with truly excellent cultures go above and beyond, like Chase's company did.

Two core principles related to trust are the following:

- Trust is counter-cultural.
- Trust is profitable.

TRUST IS COUNTER-CULTURAL

Obviously, the employees of the Enron Corporation never regained their trust in the company's leadership team—and for good reason.

Mixing scandal, hubris, and boldfaced lies will have that effect on people. (Not to mention washing out the retirement packages of thousands of workers.)

But Ken Lay is not the only leader who has had to deal with a lack of trust from the members of his organization. The truth is, we all do. That's because we live in a society of distrust, and the evidence is all around us. The fact that Enron held the title of "largest bankruptcy in US history" for only eight months has not helped people trust the world of business. WorldCom folded in July of 2002 after an $11 billion accounting scandal. Then Lehman Brothers took the crown in September of 2008. The list keeps growing. Now most of us are thinking, "Who will be next?"

Recent years have seen the rise of the Tea Party movement—a grass-roots campaign based on a fundamental mistrust of government that has ballooned into a political force based on a fundamental mistrust of government.

Yet it is a mistake to assume that distrust only happens "out there" with incidents of corporate scandal, or that it can only impact organizations with billion-dollar budgets and top-heavy leadership. A poll conducted in 2010 by Maritz Research found that only 7 percent of employees strongly agree they trust senior leaders to look out for their best interest, and only 7 percent strongly agree they trust their coworkers to do so.

Here's the reality: your employees or volunteers live in a world that is saturated with distrust, and they carry it in through your doors every day.

The same poll from Maritz Research found that 58 percent of employees who had strong trust in their management were "completely satisfied" with their job—which is a lot better than the 7 percent of employees who were satisfied without strong trust in their management. Plus, 63 percent of respondents with strong trust in management said they would be happy to spend the rest of their career with their present company, while only 3 percent of employees with weak trust in their management noted that they look forward to coming to work every day.

Employees who work for an organization defined by trust feel valued, work harder, experience greater satisfaction, and do not think about leaving for someplace else. They belong, contribute, and make a difference.

TRUST IS PROFITABLE

In the corporate world, trust and profit are not mutually exclusive. Some might suggest that doing the right thing means that you have to be a pauper. The truth is that doing the right thing can be highly profitable. The presence of unshakable trust within an organization is about a lot more than warm feelings and happy thoughts. Trust is worth money, and there are figures to prove it.

A 2004 study by LogicaCMG and Warwick Business School measured what is called a "trust dividend":

> Our research analyzed 1,200 case studies of outsourcing contracts from across the world since 1990. We found that contracts with well-managed relationships based on trust—rather than stringent SLAs (service level agreements) and penalties—are more likely to lead to a "trust dividend" for both parties.
>
> Well managed outsourcing arrangements based on mutual trust can create a *20 percent to 40 percent difference* on service, quality, cost and other performance indicators over outdated power-based relationships.
>
> Total return to shareholders in high-trust organizations is *almost three times higher* than the return in low-trust organizations.

And there's more. In his book *The Integrity Dividend*, leadership expert and author Tony Simons evaluated 275 companies and found organizations that scored higher in trust among employees added 2.5 percent to a company's bottom line.[2]

The Great Place to Work Institute's annual "Best Places to Work for in America"[3] reported some very interesting discoveries by comparing the performances of organizations that made the "Best Places to Work for" list against those that did not. They found that great workplaces—those with high levels of trust, cooperation, and commitment—outperform their peers and experience as a group in the following ways:

- They have stronger long-term financial performance.
- They experience lower turnover relative to their industry peers.
- They receive more job applications than their peers.
- They boast an integrated workforce in which diverse groups of people create and contribute to a common workplace culture of benefit to all.

Our research indicates four components that go into creating trust-worthy leadership:

- dependability
- communication
- learning
- integrity

DEPENDABILITY

The Duke University Blue Devils are one of college basketball's greatest teams. The reason: Duke's legendary "Coach K," Mike Krzyzewski, who has guided the fortunes of the Blue Devils for nearly two decades. Coach K's philosophy is simple: "Our kids have really believed in us. . . . We trust one another." Where does that trust come from? Only one source, says Coach K: Honesty. His greatest accomplishment, he says, is not getting his team to the Final Four or coaching them to a national championship. Rather, his greatest sense of accomplishment comes when "that kid who plays here knows that I've been honest with him."

Trust is the basis of all relationships, and honesty is the basis of trust. You cannot trust someone unless you believe that person will keep a promise, be candid with you, and never betray you. The first time you discover you have been lied to, all faith is gone. It takes a long time to rebuild broken trust—if it can ever be rebuilt at all.

And that is why dependability is such a valuable component for effective leadership.

A person or organization is dependable if it can be relied upon to act in certain ways. If I do what I promise, over and over, I am considered to be trustworthy and dependable.

Dependable organizations say what they mean and mean what they say. They can be relied upon when the chips are down. In situations where other people or organizations might break their word and destroy trust, dependable organizations keep faith and maintain trust. As a result, people like working for, and doing business with, organizations that are dependable.

Here are three characteristics of dependable organizations:

- *They make promises (and keep them).* Organizations are only possible because of our human ability to make, keep, and trust promises. The US Constitution is a promise that makes our government and society possible. Churches, clubs, and corporations also have documents, handbooks, policies, and procedures that embody promises that enable people to work together in an atmosphere of trust. Imagine living in a nation, working in a company, and worshiping in a church where no one could trust any other person to keep promises.
- *They are consistent.* When a person or organization behaves in a consistent manner, others begin to know in advance what

that person will or will not do. The future becomes predictable, because it is based on a consistent track record of the past. Of course, to be successful, you must build a track record that is consistently good, not consistently poor or consistently mediocre. If you are consistently good, consistently reliable, consistently trustworthy, then you are consistently dependable.

- *They are predictable.* Consistency looks to past experience—to an organization's track record. Predictability looks to the future. When we have confidence that we can predict the behavior of a person or organization, then we have trust in that person or organization. We know we can place our faith in that organization, and we know that our faith will not be disappointed.

Trust is built by people and organizations keeping promises and by behavior that is consistent and predictable. When those qualities are absent from an organization, the result is distrust, resentment, hostility, and a sense of betrayal. Motivation and morale suffer. Organizational cohesion and esprit de corps collapse. Instead of moving toward a common goal, members of the organization think, "Every man for himself!" Success is rarely achieved in a dog-eat-dog environment. Success thrives on unity, and unity feeds on dependability and trust.

Without being paternal, great organizations take care of their people, whatever the cost. They always keep their word, always commit to the highest appropriate levels of transparency, disclose as much as legally possible, and—in times of need—go above and beyond to serve and care for their people.

We chose the wording in our survey question with a great deal of intentionality. *Management can be counted on to come through when needed.* Great organizations do more than the minimum. They come through for their people. This involves a number of virtues, chief among which is that leaders bear the brunt for their people.

Leaders do not blame people for shortcomings—they are accountable themselves. They do not scapegoat colleagues to climb the ladder—they are deeply committed to the team's success. They do not provide just enough resources—they give their teams more than they need to get the job done whenever possible. In tough economic times, leaders will take the first pay cuts themselves.

Rick works for a faith-based not-for-profit as a project manager. When we asked him to describe what it was like to work there, he was expansive.

"You know, the economy is in a tough place and when that happens charitable giving—the giving this organization depends on—goes down. It can be pretty scary. Our donor base isn't a wealthy one. We are a fairly new organization without an endowment or a lot of deep-pocketed contributors.

"So times have been tough and a little scary. But one thing we do have are some seriously great leaders. These men and women are not only upbeat, they are personally encouraging of all of us. They tell us to keep on mission, bolster our faith, and set the pace themselves.

"I'm not supposed to know this, but I do. We weren't going to make payroll one time last quarter. But I got my paycheck and I am just sort of a guy around here, with no special position or a lot of responsibility. All of my friends got their paychecks too. I found out why. The three top leaders here didn't take a paycheck for two straight pay periods."

COMMUNICATION

One of our clients had gone to work for her organization right out of college, inspired by the organization's mission and integrity. The organization was committed to caring for economically disadvantaged children, many in physical danger, in some of the most treacherous parts of the world.

She accepted that the hours would be long, the pay not comparable to what many of her classmates would command, the results sometimes long in coming. None of that mattered much to her—she was on fire, on mission.

When she engaged us for executive coaching, the fire had nearly died out. It was not because of the pay or the hardships or the deferred results, but because her leaders never seemed to be able to tell her what they were going to do next or what they expected of her.

"Everyone here is all in, on mission, ready and expecting hardship. But we have to know that our leaders care enough about us to include us. When initiatives change every quarter, when policies seem to change by the week, it's hard to know what to do, when to engage, and when just to keep your head down. They just need to communicate with us and we'd do almost anything they asked!"

Communication is all about how well the organization does three things:

1. manages information
2. communicates direction
3. clarifies expectations

Every organization needs an internal information manager, whether or not that is their sole job description or just part of it. This person is not the one who knows "where the bodies are buried," but the one who makes sure that those who need to know, understand what they need to do.

She is a trusted partner and teammate, and the leaders of the organization are committed to making sure she has the flexibility and freedom to get all but the most sensitive information out to as broad an audience as necessary.

Organizations that excel in this area deploy systems such as digital employee newsletters, town hall meetings, and carefully considered "office hours" where everyone has access to leaders. More important than these tactical structures is a commitment from leaders at all levels to make sure that their direct reports feel fully informed and included.

Such confidence is contagious. In nonprofit environments, churches, and charitable organizations this is even more important. Volunteers, who have other jobs or commitments, need to have access to information 24/7.

Such information is not simply data. It is directive.

Employees and volunteers long for direction, are eager to be led, and want to know where the organization is going and how their efforts will help it get there.

In terms of communication there may be nothing more important a leader can do than make sure that everyone in the organization has a serious and growing understanding of how what they do every day impacts and influences the organization as a whole. If workers can put two and two together, they can endure cyclical downturns, resource scarcity, and even emotionally tough seasons because they feel connected to a greater purpose.

"It can be hard to discern the line between a simple miscommunication and a lie," sighed our client.

This is especially important when it relates to people who desire deeply to find meaning in their work beyond just their tasks.

Here is a diagnostic question for you as a leader: do your people, when they show up each day, have a clear sense of what they need to do to fulfill their assignment and advance the mission of the organization?

This is vastly different from a to-do list. This is a missional checklist.

When we look at the life and ministry of Jesus, his tasks could differ greatly from day to day but they were all driven by a sense of intentional mission, because He knew what was expected of Him. "My desire is to do the will of Him who sent me."

One of the most helpful leadership tools we have found is "managing expectations."

It is a bit of a strange phrase because, after all, expectations can tend to be emotional things, and managing is nothing if not rational.

But the concept is incredibly helpful. It contains the idea that expectations are important, universal, and often unstated. And it encourages the practice of actually talking about these things.

The reality is that we have unmanaged expectations in every arena of our lives—friends, family, church, and work. It is wise and good to talk about expectations ahead of time, before the pressures and stress of life combine to result in disappointment and disillusionment.

The best premarital counselors will often have their clients make a list titled "Things I Expect" and then have the couple compare the lists with the counselor. The results are both humorous and revealing.

Most employees and volunteers are asking of their leaders, with a good heart, "What do you expect of me?" What is in bounds, what is out of bounds, what will define a successful outcome, and how can I make my best contribution?"

The very best organizations are geared around making expectations crystal clear, and they do so in a systematic, intentional way.

LEARNING

There has been lots of talk about the "learning organization" in recent years, but all too little clarity about what a learning organization actually is.

There are two primary elements, we believe. The first is that an organization itself learns—it sets up systems, processes, and structures that insure that the organization is availing itself of best practices and benchmarking in its industry and that, as importantly, it is learning from its own mistakes.

But in terms of a culture characterized by employee engagement, the learning organization helps its own people be lifelong learners—in the arena of their job description, to be sure, but also in allied disciplines. The most engaged employees have told us through the years that they have a sense that their leaders value them as people with valuable minds. This is more than transactional—we will provide you with chances to learn so that you can do a better job for us. It is much more relational—we value you as a person and so we will invest in you.

In addition, the best learning organizations ensure that they have systems in place to encourage several specific behaviors: appropriate risk, problem solving, initiative, and personal development.

APPROPRIATE RISK

The least engaged workers we have come across often tell us that they feel like they are limited and constrained in their ability to take chances in their work. "Just keep your head down and do your job," seems to be the implicit message. It is only the highest levels of leadership who have the freedom to risk. Your job is to be a worker bee.

But people are not made that way, and this is no way to build a winning culture. The business literature is rife with examples of great leaders who made substantial mistakes early in their careers. Sometimes those mistakes—such as rushing a product to market too early or rushing the wrong product to market—can cause career detours. But in notable examples a young leader had a mentor or leader who acknowledged the mistake but offered a second chance bolstered by hard lessons learned.

When this happens, confidence is built and real innovation can happen.

One of our clients, in a midmanagement position in his late twenties, spearheaded the development and offering of a new service provided by his company. His managers invested capital, time, and attention to make it happen, and he was poised to profit, both professionally and financially.

For a variety of reasons, the service did not gain traction in the marketplace, and the company lost both momentum and money.

Our client assumed he would be terminated or, at best, had hit the ceiling in his progress within that company. Quite the contrary.

The company's president drew him aside, saying, "Justin, we believed in what you were putting together and we supported you. Because you were given the reins of the project, your name is attached to its failure and we know that's tough. But you're not alone. We still believe in you. Your main task now is to learn why we failed with the new service and help us put steps in place to insure it won't happen again."

Immediately after, Justin was given another significant assignment, and over the next decade rose within the company. He points to both the failure and his leader's response to it as key components in a career that, 20 years later, has been characterized by appropriate risks that have paid off more often than not.

PROBLEM SOLVING

Some people enjoy setting goals and accomplishing them. Other people enjoy solving problems. It seems that most of us excel in one or the other discipline.

Problem solvers are of incalculable benefit to organizations, but often they are not honored because they are seen as too cautious or even naysayers. What is really happening is that their problem-solving brain is seeing ahead, anticipating challenges, and kicking into gear.

Wise leaders know to look for this trait and ensure that every layer of management, really every project team within an organization, is staffed with people with the gift of problem solving. While it is often the visionary goal setters who rise to prominence, talent scouts and people pickers ought to consider the fact that, in a real sense, leaders spend their days solving problems.

Read the memoirs of any US president and you will see this theme emerge again and again. Men elected based on their vision and plans for the country's future find that what they must contend with day to day are problems to solve. After all, nothing ever reaches a president's desk unless everyone else has failed to solve or deal with it.

INITIATIVE

Our survey has told us through the years that the most engaged people feel as if they have a lot of room to "play" within their work.

Rather than being task-driven drones, their new ideas were accepted, and they were given freedom to chase them down and bring them to fruition.

"Stay in your lane" is not a phrase heard often in organizations with a great culture. "Find or invent new lanes" is!

It is hard for leaders and managers in their fifties and above to do this, we have found. If they are in a position of prominence, they have demonstrated certain behaviors that have gotten them there, and the assumption is that those behaviors should work for everyone else. It is a hard discipline to encourage initiative—more than one career is on the line! But it is a necessary discipline.

Recently we were consulting with a national Christian ministry that was lamenting the fact that it had a shortage of leaders in their twenties. For a while they batted around ideas for programs and initiatives that would "reach" this younger generation.

Out of the blue, one of the group members stopped the proceedings cold.

"Look around the room, folks. What do you see? Everyone here is in their forties and fifties. If we knew how to start initiatives which would reach twenty-somethings, we'd have done it by now!"

The discussion shifted quickly from initiating new programs to putting together a plan to identify, equip, and unleash young leaders in their networks who were in their twenties and to let these leaders take the reins in very significant areas.

It was a risky proposition and one that involved both self-awareness and humility on the part of the older leaders. But it was the right one, and is already paying dividends within that organization.

PERSONAL DEVELOPMENT

We have already written a fair amount about how an organization can invest in its people, but it is worth repeating this key point: our research indicates that the most engaged people feel that they are valued beyond their utility to the organization.

"I get a sense that they really care about me as a person" is almost a litany with engaged employees.

One of the easiest ways to communicate this care is by providing time and resources for team members to grow and learn in areas related not only to their work but also to their passions.

Let us be honest—not everyone will have their dream job in life. Probably fewer will have it than will not.

But wise organizations with great cultures will give their people great opportunities to grow and stretch, whether this is by paying for community college classes, offering in-house retreats and seminars, or even paying for employees to take a day and explore a personal passion. Work is work, but there are ways leaders can introduce the element of play!

INTEGRITY

We are not fans of American Apparel as a company. Their clothes may be okay, but they have chosen to cultivate a marketing image that is hypersexual, and some would even argue soft-core pornographic.

American Apparel's image is an extension of the personal brand of its brilliant but troubled founder, Dov Charney. Charney has encouraged a "hook-up" of sexual frankness and experimentation, even boasting of his numerous sexual relationships within the company.

It is the kind of behavior and language that would get you summarily fired at most companies. But American Apparel's board for years turned a blind eye to its founder's excesses because the company was wildly profitable.

That is, until mid-2014, when the board made moves to dismiss Charney. The problem was not the CEO's sexual misbehavior, but rather his integrity. The board discovered that Charney had misled them about financial matters and acted quickly to terminate him.

This shows us that even in organizations with values we do not share, trust is foundational.

There is no greater possession each of us has than our integrity.

And there is no organizational trait more important to a great culture than corporate integrity.

We believe that people do not leave organizations. They leave leaders. People will give up secure positions with great compensation if they do not find their leaders trustworthy.

And they will endure below-market compensation and less than ideal work environments to work for a manager they can trust.

You simply cannot have a great culture unless your people find that their leaders have integrity. Someone has defined integrity as who you are when no one is looking. I do not think we could say it any better than that.

Integrity has both an individual and a collective aspect.

Engaged employees tell us that their leaders—both those to whom they report directly and the most senior leaders at their organization—"walk the talk." They are people who are clear about their values and live those values out. Thus, when they explain the expectations they have of their people, their people are willing to commit their own integrity.

Not to walk the talk breeds cynicism, mistrust, and team members who feel that they have been given tacit permission to cheat, lie, and steal. As the service-profit chain teaches us, this has a direct impact on productivity and profitability.

The collective dimension is illustrated in our survey answer: "Our customers know what this organization stands for." Without exception, engaged employees answer in the affirmative.

What this means is that an organization's products and services must be congruent with its stated core values. If they are not, employees will be the first to know and the last to invest deeply of themselves.

In one focus group we were conducting at a brokerage, an employee spoke bitterly. "Look, the deal here is that they drill the core value statement in us, but all of us in this room know that those are just words laminated in a cheap frame on the wall in the break room."

After saying this he looked around the room as if to challenge his colleagues to disagree. In response, they looked away, studied their fingernails, or shifted uncomfortably in their chairs. This was a room full of employees disengaged because the brokerage lacked integrity. This was an organization with a poisoned culture.

So, wise leaders will do both a personal and a collective inventory, asking questions like these:

- Would the people who work for me say I walk my talk?
- Am I clear on my own personal values and do I live them out?
- Are others clear on my personal values?
- Do the products and services we offer the marketplace match up to what we say are our core values?
- When we say things like "our biggest asset is our employees," do we actually behave as if that is true?
- Does the way we treat customers, clients, and vendors comport with what we say we believe as an organization?

Integrity is hard won and, once lost, is very difficult to recover. Better to never lose it. You cannot have trust without integrity.

Trust is the foundation of all relationships. It is critical to marriages, friendships, covenants between people, contracts between entities, and agreements between countries. Without it, it would be impossible to have any social functioning whatsoever. While trust is an ingredient, it is still not the secret sauce.

SECTION TWO

THE SECRET SAUCE . . . CREATING CULTURE

5

GETTING IT ALL LINED UP

TWO YEARS LATER

Gage was excited to be heading back to the mountains of North Carolina to see his friend Chip. They had run into each other several times over the last two years, but Gage had taken no formal lessons since then. That week of lessons two years earlier had paid off.

In fact, the lessons had gone so well that Gage was now a respectable golfer, with a 15.3 handicap index, driving the ball more than 220 yards off the tee. The game had become a source of fun and relaxation to him.

And his business had thrived as well. His restaurant chain had become a regional powerhouse, his line of sauces was selling well in specialty food markets, and he was a constant presence on the Food Network, both highlighting his own cuisine and exploring the backroads of North and South America for great sauces with regional flair.

He had more money than he had ever dreamed of, people seemed to enjoy working with and for him, opportunities abounded. He was now married, with a kid on the way.

His mom had passed away, unexpectedly, a few months earlier. He had never anticipated how difficult that would be. Apart from that, life had been good for the most part. He had realized the dreams he had working in his mom's restaurant kitchen, his "living room," and then some. On certain days, the really good ones, he could still smell the aroma wafting from her kitchen.

But when he was honest with himself, often in the solitude of a hotel room, something was still missing. That last question from Chip had haunted him: who do you need to be, Gage? Over the last couple of years, he had learned to push that question aside. He stayed busy with work, family, and travel. But when he was alone, in those hotel rooms, the question would badger him, sneaking out from the dark shadows of his mind to remind him that something was terribly wrong. In those lonely moments Gage often found himself wondering whatever had happened to his father. And in those moments, tequila had become his best friend. After a couple of shots of tequila, Gage turned off the lights and shut out the question.

Even in the waking hours, Gage sensed he was stuck on a plateau. The busyness of each passing day allowed him to avoid the real question, but he knew it still lurked in the shadows. In the last few years he had sensed his creative intensity waning as he dealt with the day-to-day challenges of a growing enterprise. Sure, he had great people around him lining out financial practices and strategic imperatives. But he knew there was something slightly off-kilter.

In the beginning, food for Gage was about love and passion. Cooking took him back to his mother's kitchen and the joy he found there, bantering with the staff and cooks. And the aroma from the kitchen always seemed to ground him in reality, beckoning back to the days when he and his mom would fight, argue, and then hug. Something about the aroma from mom's kitchen was so reassuring.

His signature sign-off phrase on his TV shows was "It's all about the sauce!" and for him that served as a metaphor for life. Life was meant to be lived, savored, laced with love and joy.

But as the business grew he found himself feeling the passion less, wondering at times if the passion he felt was compatible with a large enterprise. There were times he considered selling his brand to someone else and starting all over again with a small, intimate restaurant. He was still self-assured, but he was a far cry from the brash persona he had been when he had first met Chip.

Deep inside, he wondered if he was that much further along as a leader.

Plus, he had hit a brick wall with his golf game.

On the surface, he was back in North Carolina to meet with Chip to figure out a way to shave a couple of strokes off of his average score, but as he pulled once again into the country club parking lot, he reflected that he was really looking to his coach for some life wisdom.

Chip met Gage in the parking lot with a warm handshake and a broad smile. The pro still carried himself with the same vigor and energy that Gage remembered from their first encounter.

After a good time catching up over steaming cups of coffee, Chip and Gage made their way to the practice range, where they had spent many hours a decade earlier. In the clubhouse, Gage had caught Chip up on his progress as a golfer, the recent stagnation in his game, and made it clear he was here for a tune-up and to break through to the next level as a player.

Gage pulled the cover off of his expensive driver, stood over the ball, and prepared to take a few practice swings. Chip put a gentle hand on his shoulder before he could.

"Don't swing the club, Gage. Before we actually hit anything—especially with that driver that cost more than my car—let's chat for a minute.

"Gage, I am encouraged by your progress on the physical and technical level. You are a golfer now. But I am thinking it is time now to get to the heart of the game."

Gage was intrigued. "Sounds great, Chip! What do you mean?"

Chip smiled and clasped his hands together. "What do you think is the most important part of the golf swing, Gage?"

"That's easy, it's all about torque and a compact backswing and power as you hit the ball from the inside out at downswing, right?"

Chip half-smiled. "Wrong, my friend."

Gage stepped back from the tee and lowered his club. "What is it, then?"

"Gage, most everything that is important about the golf swing takes place before the golf club is swung.

"No matter how smooth your backswing, no matter how powerful and precise your downswing, none of that matters unless you have your posture and grip correct. Before you even think about swinging a club, your fundamentals have to be correct.

"Think about it for a minute. Only a few very people in the world have the ability to stand on a football field and run 40 yards in 4.4 seconds, which is what it takes to be an elite player. Only a very few people have the ability to spring from a basketball court and hit a three-point shot with a very large person trying to block their shot who is so close they can tell what flavor of gum he is chewing.

"But anyone who has the use and control of all their limbs can stand at a driving range like this one and have the correct posture and hold the golf club correctly. It's within reach for everybody. But even if you are a great golfer or gifted athlete, unless you get those two fundamentals— posture and grip—correct, you are not going to be able to hit a good golf shot."

Gage thought for a few moments. "I remember the first time we hit the range all those years ago, you talked about the importance of posture and grip. And I get that. I've tried to incorporate those lessons through the years. For a few years there I had the habit of checking my posture every time I passed a mirror.

"But I haven't spent a lot of time thinking about those things lately, to be honest. Shouldn't they be second nature by now, doc?"

"You would think so, Gage," Chip responded. "And, surely you have a better grasp on them than when we first met. But in my years of teaching, a common theme has been that we tend to forget the basics. And when we do, our golf game stagnates, and often even regresses. So, when someone comes to me like you have today and says that their game has hit a plateau, that is the first thing I look for. As you stepped up to the ball, before you even swung the club, I saw the problems.

"Let me ask you this, Gage. When you think about why you are not playing as well as you would like, what do you believe the problem to be?"

"That's easy, Chip. There's only one thing it could be. I'm not swinging the club well."

"You'd think so. Right, Gage?" Chip said with a laugh. "But think about it this way. Unless your posture and grip are correct—unless your fundamentals are right—you can have the best hand-eye coordination in the world and your results will be poor.

"So, how about it—let's check that posture and grip, shall we?"

THE FUNDAMENTALS OF CULTURE—FROM WHAT TO HOW

You've been with us on a journey of seeing *what* organizational culture is and why it is so important. Now it is time to talk about *how* to develop that culture, how to begin cooking the secret sauce that is going to make your organization truly exceptional!

We'll start with the fundamentals. In the same way that the correct posture and grip are both important for the golf shot, there are some basics to developing organizational culture that cannot be ignored.

We call this core alignment. It is when the basics of your organization—its processes, people, and systems—are in alignment with each other. If any one of these elements is off or out of sync, the organization cannot succeed to its fullest capacity.

Remember Chip's words to Gage. You can be the finest athlete with the most elegant swing, but if your feet are pointed the wrong way or your grip is too strong or too weak, the result may be a shot that goes out of bounds or flies the green.

Same thing with your organization. You may have the best people, the finest product, the keenest grasp of your market, and the most innovative processes, but if core alignment is out of whack, there will be trouble!

Consider this diagram:

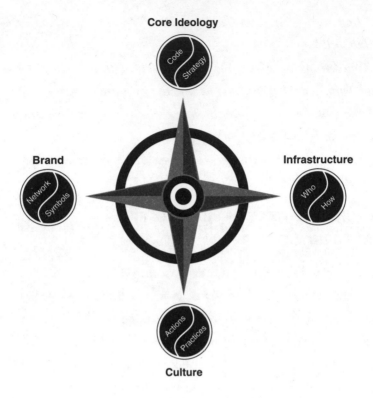

This is a picture of core alignment, illustrating its component parts. This holds true whether or not you are a manufacturing firm, a human services agency, a church, or a service provider. Whether your business is manufacturing pole vaulting equipment or developing disciples in a church, core alignment is absolutely critical.

The elements of core alignment are Core Ideology, Infrastructure, Culture, and Brand. Let us consider each in turn.

CORE IDEOLOGY

An organization's Core Ideology has two components, code and strategy.

Think of your organization's code as your DNA—the stuff that makes you you! It is a combination of core values and mission. We could make this formulaic and say that code = values + mission. But code is deeper than that. It is not that simple. Values and mission emerge from code. They support code. But over time, the core values and mission of any organization can, and should change.

Code is the essence of an organization. It has to do with its history, values, practices, assumptions, memories, heroes, and stories. It is the stuff that makes an organization what it is. It is the filter that, over time, gently or abrasively, removes everything that is not true to the essence of the organization.

It is essential to understand—even to "crack"—your organization's code so that you can leverage it for good. So, what goes into code?

Myths are the key stories that give shape to your organization and its history. Myths—which may be completely true, by the way—can be key moments when the survival of the enterprise was on the line or decision points where leaders had to be true to their values even if to do so did not appear to make short-run sense.

Traditions are collective activities that are ingrained in the organization, even if they may not appear to be essential to the corporate mission. Think of a church that is invested in a 30-year tradition of a Christmas cantata or of an Internet-based business that has pizza every Friday afternoon no matter what.

Heroes are those people who symbolize all by themselves the essence of an organization—larger-than-life figures who embody the heart and soul of a group.

Decisions are those turning point moments in the past that may have appeared routine at the time. Looking back, though, it is clear to everyone that they were pivotal moments. The time the founder decided to give added responsibility to the person who ended up becoming the next leader. The time the board turned down an apparently attractive buyout offer. Or the time the church elders decided to build a strategic addition to the church campus.

Visuals are the outer face of an organization. Think furnishings, architecture, logos, graphics, e-mail signature lines. All say something important about code.

What about your organization? We would encourage you to take a few moments and consider each of these elements. What are your myths and traditions? Who are your heroes? What have been the key decision points in your history? What does the way your organization looks, tell us about you?

What is your code?

Now, how about your strategy?

STRATEGY

Strategy is the intentional allocation of resources, to fulfill your mission, in light of your ever-changing context. It is about how you will differentiate yourself from your competitors. It is about how you will create value for your customers or beneficiaries.

Here is a truth that bears paying attention to: anyone can operate efficiently and still go out of business! An effective strategy—a key fundamental—is essential to the surviving and thriving of the enterprise.

Think of a church located in an area where there are many young families. If the church majors in ministry, music, and methods that appeal to Grandpa and Grandma, it may do those things well but be strategically ineffective. Strategy takes the realities of the marketplace and the competencies of the organization and leverages both to get results.

We have been fascinated by the San Francisco-based skin care company Rodan + Fields. For one thing, their results of late have been impressive. From 2010 to 2013 they enjoyed tenfold revenue growth.

We are also compelled by their simple, yet powerful mission: "Changing skin and changing lives." They believe you can do both and that one goes with the other.

Founded in 2002 by Dr. Katie Rodan and Dr. Kathy Fields, the company was all about bringing dermatology-based skin care to everyone. Their top-selling product was originally available only through high-end department stores, such as Nordstrom. But to fulfill their vision, they realized that they could not reach their intended audience when they were limited to department stores. So they exited the stores and headed for a direct sales approach.

Several years ago, their CEO, Lori Bush, had to make an important decision—it was one of those pivotal moments.

Rodan + Fields used a direct-selling marketing approach, and for many years had a strategy typical of such businesses. Sales representatives were rewarded for having as many other salespeople in their channel as possible—the premium was on recruiting a large team who would sell more product for the company. The compensation and incentive structure was based around this.

But as Bush looked at her people, she noticed that there were many good folks who were not selling enough to make a measurable difference in their lives—and, remember, part of the company's value proposition is "changing lives."

She began to study new employees who were succeeding to see what made them different, what was making things work for them. She reasoned that the best way to grow the company as a whole and to accomplish the aim of changing lives was to apply these best practices by investing in "behavioral training" for sales. It would not be just about "layers" of salespeople anymore.

Other executives were not so sure. The company had been pretty successful doing things the way they always had, using the traditional compensation and incentive models.

Bush faced a dilemma. She was convinced her emerging strategy would work. But she also valued her people and realized that if she was not careful, she could blow the company's code and create widespread turmoil in her people. After all, organizational history is full of examples of a credible strategy implemented in the wrong way and at the wrong time doing great damage to an organization.

So, Bush made the decision to experiment. She did not do away with the traditional model entirely, but she chose places to try the new strategy out, making it clear to everyone that the company would go with what actually worked in terms of profit and in terms of fidelity to the values of changing lives by changing skin.

As we write, the company is growing like it never has before, and more and more people are seeing both their skin and their life changed. This is largely because a wise leader held true to the company's code, but introduced a new strategy.

It is important for a leader implementing a new strategic initiative—especially in an organization with a long history—to introduce change at a rate than can be tolerated. This can be challenging. After all, presumably, the leader sees things that others do not and has the broadest and deepest sense of both the external environment and the competencies of the organization. That is why they have the leader role.

But the leader does not see everything, and it is critical to balance passionate adherence to a strategy that recognizes the human dynamics that are at play in every organization. The best strategy is the one that is not only effective but is owned by folks through the organization.

Hopefully, it is becoming clear how intertwined strategy is with your organization's code. Take Rodan + Fields again. One of the endeavors the company is most passionate about is their Prescription for Change Foundation.

Its mission is to connect people with the products, knowledge, resources, and opportunities to change their skin and change their lives. The foundation, set up as a nonprofit, allows associates to invest time and the company to invest money in causes and organizations that focus on personal self-esteem and all of the issues that flow from that. The company has made a strategic decision to put its associates' time and its own money in places that are directly tied to its code and mission.

So, Rodan + Fields team members are involved in transitional housing in San Francisco, emergency human services in Nashville, alcohol and drug recovery in Detroit, and a host of other areas of great need that can be served by the company's values and mission. This is a company that, in a few short years, has learned how to create opportunities for people to belong, contribute, and make a difference. Their strategy and mission are congruent with their code.

How about your organization, whether you are the point leader, a team leader, or an aspiring leader? Do you have a coherent strategy that is true to your code and responsive by the people you are trying to reach—customers, clients, members?

INFRASTRUCTURE

Infrastructure is the second dimension of core alignment. Infrastructure involves both the *who* and the *how* or an organization.

WHO

You will not be surprised to hear that when we talk about who, we are talking about your people. In particular we are talking about the talents of your people.

In our consulting work we spend a lot of time talking about "prevailing talent."

In their book *Your Intentional Difference: One Word Changes Everything*, our colleagues Ken Tucker, Shane Roberson, and Todd Hahn write about prevailing talent at length.

Here is how they define it: your spontaneous, observable, reliable, and measurable patterns of thinking, feeling, and behaving.

Think about it in terms of your people. Each and every one of them has a very specific talent. They are known for it. "Brandon always cuts through to the essence of a problem." "Jessica always manages to bring people together, even people who don't normally get along." The very best organizations are keyed to identify, recognize, celebrate, and leverage the prevailing talents of their people.

Some of this is intuitive. But there are measures to identify talents as well, well-known ones such as Myers-Briggs Type Indicator, the DISC profile, and the Clifton StrengthsFinder. Using such instruments in leadership development initiatives is a powerful way to get people thinking in terms of and acting in line with their talent.

When organizations have formal or informal mentoring problems, we encourage both mentor and mentee to make sure they have a clear grasp of their individual talents and to orient much of the content of the mentoring relationship around developing and deploying talents.

Here is a great exercise we use to help you understand your talent and how great it is to spend most of your time using that talent. We call it the Energy Exercise.

First, think about the last time you went home at the end of a day energized and full of life. Ask yourself two questions:

1. What had you done that day?
2. What particular and individual talents had you tapped into that day in your life or work?

Now, turn the question on its head. When was the last time you finished a day drained, exhausted, maybe even a little depressed? Ask yourself three questions:

1. What had you done that day?
2. What particular and individual talents that you have were you tapping into that day?
3. What particular and individual talents that you have were you NOT tapping into that day?

If you are a leader, consider asking this question on a widespread basis—maybe in one-on-one meetings—and beginning to prioritize ways to get your people living in their talents!

But there are times when a person's talent profile does not match with the core ideology. At that point, you have core misalignment and must deal with it. A few years ago, we were coaching a service organization associated with a university in the Pacific Northwest. The university was in an urban setting. After years of decline, the organization was down to a handful of students, a couple of faculty members, one or two administrators. Bonnie, the sole staff person, struggled to lead this small group. The board brought us in to answer several questions. How do we grow the organization? How do we fund our efforts? How do we get the staff person to build a team, develop a strategic plan, and complete her reporting to the board in a timely manner? Everyone was frustrated, including Bonnie.

After examining her talent configuration, however, we realized that she needed to be part of a team. Her profile was not suited for a lone ranger position. Over the course of several weeks, we had one of the board members walk through the difficult conversation with her. She eventually resigned. Three months later, we got a call from her father, a professor at that same university, thanking us for how we handled the transition. He said that she was happier than she had been in years and was relieved that she was no longer part of such a difficult job. Was she talented? Absolutely! Was she the right person for the situation? Absolutely not! The "who" must be aligned with the organization's core ideology. In Bonnie's case, the board had not done a great job in clarifying core ideology, so she never quite knew what was expected of her. Just like tires that are misaligned on a car, organizational misalignment can wear down the most talented people and the best organizations.

HOW

If the "who" is about people, the "how" is all about processes and structures. It is about the other resources that are needed to support the core ideology. There is an old saying that "roads are paved-over cow paths." In essence, our structures typically emerge from default ways of operating, rather than by intentional design.

At TAG, we consult with several church denominations that are defined, in part, by the concept of "order." Following the Protestant Reformation, several conflicts emerged in the church related to how much latitude a pastor could have, which liturgy was correct, and how to administer the sacraments correctly. The "order" established in the sixteenth century prevails in many churches even in the twenty-first century. And for many, this is a problem.

The structures and processes that were created to address a particular set of issues in the 1500s still drive operations today in many mainline churches. The churches that are thriving in today's context are typically the ones that are driven by core ideology, rather than structure, and they continually align their processes and structures to that core ideology. The "how" must change as often as the strategy changes.

The same is true for businesses and government agencies. In many cases, yesterday's structures are limiting today's success. Put another way, yesterday's solution has become today's problem. Laws enacted by Congress to address particular issues have unintended negative consequences. Corporate policies intended to protect the company end up violating employee trust.

To create alignment, you must constantly evaluate your processes and structures to ensure that you are preserving your code and updating your strategy. The status quo is tenacious. In golf, poor posture and a weak grip do not typically happen overnight. Bad habits creep in over time. The same is true for any organization's infrastructure.

CULTURE

The third dimension of core alignment is Culture.

In a sense, our whole book is about culture, but it is important to see culture in relationship to other components of organizational effectiveness. "Culture eats strategy for lunch," goes the saying, and we believe it.

But that is not to say that strategy is unimportant. In fact, to understand core alignment you have got to see that culture and strategy fit together, like posture and grip in golf!

We see two dimensions to culture—our Practices, and our Actions.

PRACTICES

Practices are our intentional behaviors. They are the things we set out to do. Rodan + Fields people set out not to move product but to change lives, and this is reflected in their language. From its earliest days, Southwest Airlines has been about "love," and so their people consciously try to love each other and their customers. A friend of ours who owns a bagel shop in Charlotte shows up for work before dawn each morning deliberately trying to replicate the process of bagel making his father used on the Lower East Side.

Years ago, there was a commercial featuring the golfer Tiger Woods. The camera panned through his house and showed rain coming down in sheets outside—a Florida gully washer! Tiger's voice-over talked about taking days off and resting…what most of us would do if we were a golfer and there was a veritable tsunami. But as the commercial ended, the camera panned outside, to the practice range behind Tiger's house, where he was hitting shot after shot in the pouring rain.

Every organization has these practices. They are sourced in what you believe to be true about yourself, what you value, the talents of your people, and the demands of your clientele.

One of our clients, Memorial Drive Presbyterian Church, in Houston, practices "dollar for dollar giving," and they have done so for over 50 years. With a budget in excess of $10 million, they give half of their money to missions. They do this in good economic times and bad, when the church can easily meet payroll or it has to stretch. It is just part of who they are.

Practices have to do with the "things we do around here" that are unique to your organization. This is what distinguishes you from all others. One of our first clients, a private bank in Charlotte, had prospective tellers participate in as many seven interviews before they were offered a job. This created a culture of expectation.

"If I have to go through seven interviews, including one with the board chair, this must be a special place to work," is what one teller told us.

Another client, The Cardiovascular Group of Northern Virginia, instituted a practice that prohibited their physicians from working more than four and a half days each week. This practice started 15 years ago.

According to one of their cardiologists, this very large medical practice has only experienced two divorces in the ensuing years.

Pause for a minute to think about your organization. What are the nonnegotiable things that you do on purpose?

ACTIONS

If practices are intentional behaviors, actions are unintentional behaviors. In a very real sense, we are not always aware of our actions.

Our book is about the process of forging a very intentional culture—the secret sauce is in the process. But it is important that we realize that an awful lot of culture has to do with the things we rarely think about, the way a fish regards water . . . it is just there!

Think back to American Apparel's Dov Charney. He was intentional about creating a highly sexualized culture at the company, unashamed of multiple sexual liaisons with employees, brash in conveying a brand image of unabashed eroticism.

As things unraveled in his leadership, female employees were lining up to file sexual harassment suits, against Charney and others. An unintended consequence of a sexually promiscuous culture was that people took the good gift of sex and misused it in ways that caused profound harm.

Think of the church that has a high view of the moral demands of Scripture. Its practices may include high levels of accountability and moral standards for its leaders. Its actions, though, could include unhealthy judgment and the pattern of prying closely into the lives of its congregants as a sort of "gotcha game."

It works both ways, though. A company that is very intentional about customer service will institute rigorous practices to insure that customers' needs are met unfailingly. Over time, team members will make many small decisions and take nearly unconscious actions during the day that further the value of caring for people.

There is a very distinctive and complex interrelationship between actions and practices. As it plays out, practices lead to actions more often than not, especially when the other elements of core alignment are in place.

Practicing the correct grip and posture on the golf course (a practice) will pay dividends when it comes to the plane of the backswing and downswing, and the angle at which the club face strikes the golf ball. It is almost impossible for a golfer to see the club head when it comes into contact with the ball (an action), but if the correct fundamental practices have been put into place, the result will be a good one.

BRAND

What do these all have in common?

Apple

Jeep

Star Trek

North Carolina Basketball

Notre Dame Football

In-N-Out Burgers

They are all brands. But they all go beyond a typical brand. They have each created what has become known as a "brand community." They all make you think of something, and cause most people to think of the same thing. They are identified with a fact, a person, a feeling, or an expectation. Brands are powerful. Your organization has one, whether or not you have been intentional about it. In the minds and hearts of your customers, congregants, or clients you are identified with something or some things.

A bad brand can be an organization killer or a leverage point for success.

What do you think of when you read the words Harley-Davidson Motorcycles?

If it were 1983, you would have thought "on the verge of extinction." After years of being the motorcycle of choice for those who liked the open road and a little wildness in their lives, the company was on the verge of shutting its doors. Identified with danger, not fun, which was the negative impact of the Hell's Angels biker gang, coupled with an aging customer base, Harley desperately needed an infusion of brand awareness.

The company made a decision that turned its fortunes around (25 years later its brand was valued at $7.8 billion and was considered one of the 50 strongest in the world) and created a revolution in marketing circles. It created a brand community.

A brand community is a group of passionate customers or consumers who identify so strongly with a brand that they will organize chunks of their life around it.

Apple fans must have every new gadget Cupertino puts out. Jeep fans compare notes on photos of prototype models online months before they are available for sale. English Premier League soccer fans decorate their homes in team colors.

Brand communities make sense in our world. There is a real sense of craving for community. Remember, we are basing our work on the idea that people want to belong, contribute, and make a difference. In addition, in tighter economic times, an organization that can create a strong community around its products or services is doing less with more.

There is a lot of good literature on creating brand communities, but let us focus on two key components. Developing a brand community requires a commitment from the whole organization, not just the marketing arm, and developing a brand community is about getting involved in people's lives, not just selling to them.

It is not enough to say, "Hey, let's create a brand community— sounds like a good marketing strategy!" The entire organization must be committed. When Harley-Davidson adopted a brand community strategy to save the company, this commitment was reflected in everything from its organizational structure (the company got rid of "silos" and flattened out management) to its internal communication processes, to the way it interacted with the community through its great tradition of community service activities.

This latter example points out how important relationship-building is in creating a brand community. For years, Harley-Davidson had hosted elaborate and genuinely helpful community service events. But, for the most part, outsiders and other professionals were called upon to staff these events. As its brand community strategy unfolded, Harley made the decision to have its own employees staff the events, face to face and shoulder with its customers and potential customers.

The results were profound. Employees became riders, employees understood their customers better, people who had not previously considered riding became raving fans. The organization said to its constituency, "We care about you and your life, and making it better, not just about selling you a product."

Those little Goldfish crackers are addictive, aren't they? You would think little kids would be a natural brand community for Goldfish. But when the company that makes Goldfish tried to create a suite of online interactive games for kids on its website, the effort flopped. Kids would rather eat Goldfish than play games about them.

Then the company became aware of devastating statistics about depression and low self-esteem among children. Its customers and potential customers were struggling with some pretty traumatic things. So, it pulled the Goldfish games and began creating conversations and initiatives around getting kids the help they need.

The message? "Yes, we would love for you to buy our tasty little crackers. But, even more important, we want to add value to your life." Kids responded, parents responded gratefully, and the Goldfish brand rocketed in value.

What could it mean for your organization to create a brand community? Many of our readers work in the faith arena. Churches and not-for-profit organizations that serve the community are ripe to generate brand communities! What are you known for? Who is already flocking to you? Who are your biggest fans?

Now, how can you strengthen your connection with yourself and their connection with each other? It is good business, and it is good for business to do so.

We have covered a lot of ground in talking about core alignment. Hopefully, we have given you some practical applications and reflection exercises for your leadership and your own organization. Core alignment is a factor in what allows people to belong, contribute, and make a difference.

But, as important as it is, core alignment is not the secret sauce.

6

WHEN YOU'VE LOST YOUR SAUCE

A year later, Gage was judging a cooking contest at Johnson and Wales University in Charlotte, so he made the short drive to the mountains to see his friend Chip. As he made the drive up to the club he was doing some honest reckoning with himself. Even though, by all standards, his business was still profitable, he was still feeling that sense of discontent that he couldn't explain.

In addition to refocusing his golf game on his posture and grip, he had refocused his company through an alignment process. They were clear on their values and mission. The brand was thriving and his employees seemed engaged, at least from what he could tell. But something still wasn't quite right.

This puzzled him deeply, because he was tantalizingly close to having everything he had ever wanted—financial resources, a loyal staff team, fame, something approaching an "empire." His sauce still sold well, even though there were new competitors taking large chunks of market share. But, by anyone's standards, he was still a success.

And after all that work on grip and posture, even his golf game was improving!

But this time Gage was not interested in talking to Chip about golf. It was too cold to play in the winter months anyway. He was more concerned with his sense of malaise and what that might mean. He wondered if he was missing something or needing a new direction entirely.

It was eight degrees on the mountain, with the wind chill well below zero, and when Gage got out of his car to head to the clubhouse he breathed deeply, clearing his head and collecting his thoughts to present to Chip. He bounded up the steps into the warm clubhouse and looked around for Chip.

As usual they met in the grill room. In the offseason, it was a very quiet place. Snow covered the golf course below, while the fireplace twinkled across the room, so coffee was a necessity. They also ordered lunch. While Chip rec-ommended the barbecue sandwich, soaked in an Eastern North Carolina vinegar-based sauce with a scoop of coleslaw on top, Gage ordered a Club sandwich. Like many gifted chefs, Gage believed that a well-executed Club sandwich was a culinary art form. With a mole spread, instead of the typi-cal aioli, Gage wondered if the chef had prepared a tribute of some sort.

As they finished catching up and Gage nibbled the last of his house-made chips, he got down to business.

"Here's the deal, Chip. I'm successful and, between you and me, worth a small fortune now. This is what I started out dreaming of years ago. But something is unsettled in me and I can't figure it out. I was wondering if you could help me think it through."

Chip thought for a long moment before replying.

"Gage, I know your company is doing well and the signs are all good, but are you as protected as you think? I mean, not to be brash, but I am hearing about a lot of other sauces eating into your market space."

Gage looked surprised, and Chip smiled.

"Yes, ever since we have become friends, I have become a bit of a foodie. And I've read an article about you here and there. Plus, our chef here at the club just returned from a conference where everything focused on the sauce."

Gage took a deep breath.

"You know, you may be onto something. Our team doesn't want to face this because we are going full steam ahead and doing well, but I don't know that we have the unique niche or the energy we once did. Our competitors may be catching up to us because we may be getting a bit complacent.

"We're making a lot of money, and because of your help the team is focused and energized and happy, but what's interesting is we're focused on very different things than we used to be. And while the company is thriv-ing, I feel like I'm not. A few years back, as I anticipated this season of life, I thought I would be the happiest that I could possibly be."

Chip looked at Gage intently and then asked him, "Gage, how do you spend your time?"

Gage thought for a moment then said, "I guess about half of it is in management meetings and the other half is with the public."

Chip continued. "When was the last time you were in the kitchen? When was the last time you actually cooked your sauce?"

Gage then confessed, "I realized on the drive up here that I actually haven't thought about the sauce in a while. I mean the actual sauce. *I am so focused on the corporate side of things—investors, personnel, facilities—that I hardly ever make it to the test kitchen anymore. Isn't that weird? When I started this deal, I never wanted to leave the kitchen and I had to hire all of these corporate types to run the ship so we could make a profit. We followed your advice, Chip. We created alignment.*

"Now I am one of those corporate types. And I'm pretty damn good at it. But I am certain that I have to be that *corporate guy if this thing is going to succeed. I trust my people, but this company needs hands-on leadership from the top."*

"Gage, listen to me for a minute," Chip interrupted. "The best golfers love golf. They may have to work a cash register at a pro shop every week. They may spend time on the range perfecting their game. But a true golfer lives on the course. I think you've spent too much time behind the cash register, Gage."

"There's only one reason you would feel the way you do," Chip continued.

Gage looked at him, lost. "I feel like I've lost something."

"You have. You've lost something very critical," Chip replied.

Gage's silence invited Chip to continue.

"Let me ask you a question, Gage. Tell me about your mother."

Gage leaned back in his chair and chuckled. "Oh, so now you are Sigmund Freud? Are you going to ask about my dad next or invite me to lay on that comfy couch in the clubhouse and talk about my childhood?"

Chip smiled but continued.

"No, it's about mission. When I first got to know you, you were full of stories about what it was like to grow up in your mother's restaurant kitchen, interacting with the chefs, experimenting with spices, learning

how she made her famous mole sauce, even fighting with her over priorities and values.

"Something got ingrained in you then, a love and passion for food and cooking and the life of a chef. The long hours, the hard work, the standing on your feet for hours, the uncomfortable temperatures. You actually loved all of that—the sights, sounds, the heat, and most of all the aroma.

"And your company was born out of that aroma, out of that passion. It was all about the sauce, as you said countless times. It was about creating a caliente culture. It was about giving the people who ate your food an unforgettable experience. It was never about investors and personnel and budget decisions. It was all about the sauce.

"You've lost your way, my friend. Remember that question, that third question, that I asked you several years ago, Gage? You never answered it. Who do you need to be, Gage? Yes, your company has grown and needs highly skilled professional management. Yes, you've got great core values and mission statements and strategic priorities. But that's not what it needs, at least from you. Not right now. From you, it needs a passion for food and the experience of eating in community. Your company is doing many of the right things. But you are the wrong one to be doing them.

"Here is a truth I have discovered—ironically, when we are the most successful, we are the most vulnerable. I see this in sports all the time. Think of the many of the most talented and successful athletes over the last few years and how they lost their passion, sold out, or cheated. Barry Bonds, Lance Armstrong, Mike Tyson, Michael Vick, Mark McGwire. Not to mention the countless golfers who would make that list. Tremendous amounts of talent. . . all squandered. Yes, they have stayed in the headlines, but for all the wrong reasons.

"But, Gage, do you remember George Archer? He may be a little before your time. I got to know him at a few gatherings. He won over a dozen PGA Tour events, including the 1969 Masters. In fact, his daughter was the first female caddie in the history of the Masters. She caddied for him in 1983.

"George was even more prolific on the Senior Tour. Well, over dinner one night in Charlotte, he told me a bit of his story. As a 6'5" high

school freshman, he was projected to be a great basketball player. Colleges were starting to take notice. But his coach kicked him off his high school team after one year because he kept skipping practice... to play golf instead!

"He couldn't help but play golf every chance he got. Even after multiple surgeries throughout his career—wrist, shoulder, and even hip—he kept going back out to play. He couldn't help it. When he joined the tour in 1964, he told his wife he wanted to play five years. Instead, he told me that he'd played five careers. And he said that if he couldn't be a golfer, he would have been a caddie. His career was really a legacy of passion.

"Gage, at the end of the day, the questions you need to be asking are 'Who am I?' 'What am I doing?' 'Am I following my passion?' I mean by that, what sort of legacy do I want to leave? And, are the activities I am giving myself to do every day advancing or detracting from the opportunity I have to leave that legacy? Gage, you've lost your passion."

For a moment, feeling completely lost, Gage fell intro a trance.

Then, an aroma startled Gage out of his slumber. He turned around and caught a glimpse of the wood-burning stove in the kitchen. For the first time in years, he could smell his mother's kitchen. And just at that moment, a single ray of sunshine broke through the gray tapestry and descended on top of the snow-covered fairway.

THREE OPTIONS IN SAN CLEMENTE

One of our clients at TAG was San Clemente Presbyterian Church, in California. By all measures of success the church was doing great. Even on the cusp of a recession, they had a $100,000 surplus in their budget. Their attendance was growing. The people seemed to be happy, and the church was having a measurable impact in its community. The church had almost died in the 1990s. Then they hired an energetic, bright, charismatic leader. Not just a preacher, but a true leader. Tod Bolsinger arrived on the scene having been mentored by some of the most renowned church leaders in the United States.

But when Tod called us, he was restless. A sharp and perceptive leader, he was seeing early warning signs of disengagement. Long-time volunteer leaders were talking about "burnout." The pipeline of new leaders seemed to be drying up a bit. There was a tangible sense that energy and enthusiasm was waning. Even though the traditional markers of a church—strong attendance and finances and community involvement—were all positive, he intuited that something was wrong.

The first thing he said to us was that he did not have a vision problem. In fact, he had just fired his previous coach because that was what the coach kept telling him. Tod knew there was something else lurking in the shadows at San Clemente. And it was not a vision problem. He asked us to take a peek under the hood.

So we began a discovery process. In our discovery work at TAG, we look at organizations from every angle. We talk to people. We conduct focus groups. We do surveys and compare organizations to national norms. We analyze data, demographics, financials, and technologies. But we rarely accept the problem at face value. Most of the time, the way people frame the problem is the problem.

On the one hand, Tod had an intuitive sense that the church did not have a vision problem. At the same time, he saw that the problem was somehow a problem with the church's leadership, so he wanted answers. He wanted to know what needed to be fixed, and how to fix it.

What we found was fascinating.

The people loved the church and loved Tod (this is not always the case in our work!). In many ways, we have never encountered a church that spoke more positively of their pastor, his skills, and his leadership.

But there were indeed things going on under the hood. We kept hearing the sentiment "I love this church, but they don't really need me here. I love everything about this place, but there is really no place for me to make a difference here, to express my skills and gifting."

In fact, one guy pulled us aside and said, "I just retired as the CEO of one of the leading real estate firms in Southern California. I'd love to bring my experience to the church, but the only place where I seem to be able to help is in ushering people into pews on Sundays."

The reality was that Tod had been highly effective at bringing a unified vision to a church that, before his tenure, was lacking one. No one at the church had any doubt about why the church existed, its values, or its vision.

But, over time, a unified vision had led to a centralized institution.

Camp out with us there for a moment. Unity had led to everything being lodged in senior leadership. The sense was "this guy has done the work, brought the church back from the brink of irrelevance, has led us well for over a decade, and so now what are we needed for?" All unintended consequences—Tod was and is a highly effective leader with great values.

But the very discipline and focus that had led to shared values and mission had led to stasis—a lack of creativity and adaptability going forward. The unique nature of the church's locale in California was that it was located in a community that prized and prioritized entrepreneurialism.

It had become too "corporate."

We shared our findings with Tod, who was, understandably, pained and disturbed. We let him know there were indeed some early warning signs that needed attention. He took it all in and asked us a series of rapid-fire questions:

"What's causing this? What's at the heart of the problem? What needs to change?"

We took a deep breath and gave the hardest answer of all:

"You."

Think about that for a moment. A pastor beloved by his congregation, an effective leader, discipler, preacher, caregiver. And yet, he was the problem?

Yes.

Our conversation continued.

"Look," we said, "your people love you. You have given the congregation a new sense of hope and purpose and mission. They respond well to and respect you. But they see you as the center of the church, and that is the problem.

"There's no doubt that this is not what you want—we have gotten to know you well enough to discern that. You don't want the church to be about you. But in our discovery process what happened is that people talked more about you than anything else. And you could continue to lead the way you are, and your church would be healthier than most. But over time what will happen is that because you are seen as so central and so competent, your most creative and committed members will think that they are not needed and slowly move away.

"Unconsciously, the message that is going out is that everyone else is here to support YOUR ministry. They love you enough to sustain that for a while. But long term, it will sap the energy and mission of the church."

It was a tough message to hear, and a tough message to deliver.

But being a good and wise leader, Tod heard it and asked the right question.

"So, what is the way forward?"

We told him that there was one of three options.

Option one was that he could continue as he was. He was in the top percentile of leaders and, more than likely, the church would continue to grow, at least incrementally. But what would happen ten years or so later would be that the church would decline as it lost its energy and would enter crisis mode about the time he was leaving.

Option two was to resign. It was entirely a credible solution. It would provoke a crisis—which is often a good thing to do as a leader—because it would require the people to rediscover their mission apart from the pastor's vision. But there was a decent chance that the church might implode in that scenario.

Option three was the one we suggested: "Learn to lead differently." We proposed a less top-down and more collaborative style, with the beloved Senior Pastor less in the center of things and others stepping in. This is a risky option. We knew the pastor would experience a loss of control and perhaps a loss of significance. We knew he would lose a sense of competence derived from operating with a leadership style that had largely worked for him and produced success.

We knew that he would be criticized for abdicating authority and leadership. We knew there would be a degree of pain all around. But we also knew that it was vital that he make a courageous decision to insure the long-term vitality of the church and his own leadership.

Tod's next series of questions involved how to restructure and reorganize leadership. But we told him to avoid the temptation to restructure. That would simply distract his leadership from the real work. We said to him, "Tod, don't reorganize. Simply behave differently. Ask your staff how you, and they, can do that." He was startled, since most consultants would have jumped right into restructuring the org chart, but he eventually accepted our challenge.

In Tod's own words, he told us, "because I love my church and being their pastor, because I love the community that I live in and because I really wanted to give my family as much stability as I could, I opted pretty quickly for number 3. It wasn't easy, and frankly I didn't know what I had signed up for. The lessons my staff, lay leaders, and I would have to learn over the next several years would challenge everything we thought we knew. There were moments of profound insecurity and doubt. There were many hard decisions to make. And I would be lying if I didn't admit that quite often I wish I could just go back to the way it was, but I have been relearning what it means to lead ever since."

In the months following that decision, the staff leadership team had a new rule: don't say "no" to anything that lay people dream up. Always say yes. Let's just see what happens. The culture began changing, but most people didn't really know why. Lay leadership became more engaged. And while things are never perfect in any organization, San Clemente Presbyterian is behaving differently. And so is Tod. As we write this book, Tod has accepted a new position to teach leadership at the graduate level. He is continuing to behave differently, now influencing an emerging generation of future leaders. In fact, he has told this story to an international audience through his own book, *Canoeing the Mountains: Christian Leadership in Uncharted Territory* (Intervarsity Press, 2015).

When we think about our work with clients, we think in terms of our own motto at TAG: Reframe, Refocus, Reimagine.

We live by those words and they guide our work with clients in all of the sectors we serve. Let us unpack what they mean and how they can apply to your own life and leadership as well. Maybe there is another Tod Bolsinger reading this book.

REFRAME, REFOCUS, AND REIMAGINE

One of the most important things we can do for our clients is to help them reframe the challenges and opportunities they are facing.

Think about a picture hanging in a—you guessed it—a frame.

As long as that picture is in the frame, what is in the frame is all you will see. But what if you took the picture out and hung it on another background, with a different color backing it up? It might change the way you look at the picture itself, right?

One of our colleagues told us the story of a friend who started coming home from work later than usual. He worked for a company that restored buildings and homes that had flooded. After a few weeks, his exhaustion obvious. His wife asked him why he was coming home late so frequently. His answers were evasive and he changed the subject.

She jumped to the obvious conclusion—he was having an affair. At that point, she had him in a frame. Everything he did, she interpreted within that frame—every time he was late or tired or distracted, she assumed he was seeing another woman. She started questioning every action. They argued and fought. She started drinking heavily. Their marriage was falling apart.

But the real story was that he had always felt ashamed for never taking her on a real honeymoon. After their wedding, he immediately started working for the restoration company. So, to rectify the situation, he had taken on a second job and was working overtime to save up for a real honeymoon.

Her frame was based on her observations. Her observations, however, were based on her interpretation of the actions. And that interpretation led to her own actions and reactions: fighting, drinking, and gossiping with other underappreciated wives in her apartment complex.

Think about her actions and reactions if she had had the correct frame. She would have interpreted his actions completely differently. As a result, her responses to him would have changed as well. Instead of screaming or withdrawing or drinking heavily, based on the "affair" frame, maybe she would have started picking up some things around the house that he would normally take care of. Maybe she would have offered to drive him to work early one morning, just to spend time with him. One frame leads to a particular series of interpretations, actions, and reactions. The other frame leads to an entirely different series of interpretations, actions, and reactions. What a reframe does is allow her more options, more possibilities.

As leaders, we interpret every situation we face, and that interpretation sets the course of action for how we feel and respond. Every situation in reality tends to have multiple angles, but we get crystallized in one way of seeing things, and this is not helpful and limits our leadership options.

The frame we put on a situation often creates uncertainty and anxiety. We can only see the situation in one particular way, and the situation morphs into a problem that is unsolvable, often because the frame we have given it allows for only one path forward.

When we are introduced into a perplexing situation with a client, we have a general rule: do not accept the frame of the problem as presented. If we do, we will usually become stuck, exactly along the same lines that the organization is currently stuck.

A successful reframe must be a valid alternative perspective on the situation. It must be somewhat surprising. It has to be plausible and resonate with the person or the group, as it did with Tod Bolsinger. And as a person comes to see and understand the reframe, new solutions, new pathways will open.

Many artists spend almost as much time choosing a frame for their work as they do creating their work. They may try multiple frames. Each frame highlights a different shade, stroke, highlight, or shadow. The artist tries multiple frames until she finds that one that makes the most sense of what she is trying to convey. Sometimes, we have to try on multiple frames for our complex problems before we find the one that works. And then we have to be willing to discard the new frame if it does not create a new path forward.

Reframing, then, is looking at things from a different, more creative perspective that gives us alternative ways forward.

This is what Chip was doing for Gage in our story in the first part of this chapter. He was reframing his perception of things from "I am losing steam because I am so tired of managing the corporate side of things" to "What if I don't have to manage the corporate side of things at all? What if I can get back to my driving passion?" With that reframe, Gage suddenly has a completely different set of options open to him, which brings greater freedom and possibility for him as a leader.

When Chip brought up Gage's formative experience in his mother's restaurant, it was a classic reframe. He took Gage from thinking about his corporate tasks and responsibilities back to his first love—the smells and intensity and creativity of cooking.

In our consulting work, we have been thrust into situations where people have come up against what they perceive to be insurmountable problems. As humans, when things are not working well, we attempt to get to the bottom of things, diagnose the problem, and set things straight. Often, the diagnosis places blame with a person or a department within the organization. For example, in one organization, sales had been declining, and the sales manager was held responsible and fired. This happened to be the fourth sales manager in two years to come in, be blamed, and be fired. The organizational leadership was fixated on the sales manager position as the point of the problem.

When we came in to view the problem, we broadened our lens to include the overall functioning of the organization, especially those who directly interfaced with sales. What we found was the consistent undercutting of the authority of the sales manager by the marketing vice president, who was threatened by accelerating sales numbers and worked to sabotage whoever was in the manager position.

The way we reframed the situation to leadership was by using this old adage (attributed to a variety of sources): "Your system is perfectly designed to give you the results you're getting." The issue is not the sales manager. The issue isn't even the marketing vice president. It is the way the whole system has been designed that allows sales numbers to directly influence how the marketing vice president is evaluated in her job, and how she then is motivated to undercut the sales manager in turn.

In a different vein with Tod, we raised the possibility that the problem with his church's declining energy was actually him. This allowed him to consider how changing himself, not adopting new strategies and programs, could propel the church forward.

What in your life or organization could use a reframe right now? What are new possibilities and ways of thinking for you and those you lead and love?

THE INTERPRETATION PROBLEM

Frames come from interpretations. We all take in data—conversations, e-mails, pictures, body language. Then we interpret the data. Our interpretations come from a variety of sources—family members, news media, friends, and colleagues. But they also come from our own history, perspectives, and worldviews. When we interpret data, we then tend to act. If the interpretation is wrong, the action can become a problem.

Several years ago, we were called to work with a bank in Michigan. This was in the early days of online banking, and this particular community bank was struggling to make the transition from bricks-and-mortar to online banking. The CEO called us in and asked us to help.

So we started with a survey and some focus groups. Very quickly, we began hearing the same thing from a variety of employees: the problem was training. "This is all new to us and we need more training," they said.

Armed with that information, we checked out their Product Knowledge test scores. To our surprise, they were off the charts! They said they needed more training, but the data suggested otherwise.

After a few hours on-site, a group of employees pulled aside and told us that they knew what the *real* problem was. The real problem, they said, was that the CEO had a terrible temper. So we took the bait.

"What does it look like when he loses his temper," we asked?

"Hmmm, we've never actually seen him lose his temper. But he has a terrible temper. Take our word for it!" they shot back.

Thoroughly confused, we met with the Executive Vice President. She told us about her job. While her job description was primarily operations, she fancied herself to be the bank's "problem solver."

"I have a line outside my door on Mondays," she proudly proclaimed. "I tell the employees that if they have a problem, come to me and I'll fix it. I'm the problem solver here!"

All of a sudden, it hit us. She was communicating that she was a problem solver. For the employees, that was "data." And data needs interpretation. So their interpretation was twofold. "If we have a problem, we are incompetent to solve that problem" was the first interpretation. The second interpretation was "if we have a problem, go to her not the CEO. Therefore the CEO must not be safe. He must have a terrible temper."

Data cries out for interpretation. Interpretation demands action. Actions demand reactions. And pretty soon, people are stuck. We suggested that she try closing her door for a few months. That seemed to do the trick. But what if we had taken the prevailing interpretation? The employees need more training? Let's spend thousands of dollars on a new training program! The CEO has a bad temper. Fire the jerk and bring in someone with people skills. In either scenario, the "solution would become the problem."

FROM REFRAMING TO REFOCUSING AND REIMAGINING

While we can help our clients reframe, the task of refocusing lies within them, mostly. A refocus follows from the reframe. Once I see things differently and can imagine different possibilities, I then have the chance to reset things in a tangible way. Energy now is rechanneled away from the anxiety of a situation that is not reconciling and is continually distracting, to productive problem solving in a whole new direction.

Notice that Chip was not prescriptive for Gage. He did not tell him what to do. Only Gage can do that. But you can imagine from that conversation that a refocus for Gage will involve getting back into the test kitchen, getting away from spreadsheets, and getting back to his first love—the sauce! The reframe creates the possibilities for the refocus—the unleashing of creative energy to solve the problem in a whole new way.

The danger for Gage is that unless he refocuses, his organization could actually be in peril. Competitors are creeping into the market and although his company is still profitable and growing, it is clear that unless some things change, that is not inevitable.

What Chip was really doing for Gage was saying, "Scrape away the TV shows, the book deals, the celebrity, the 'stuff.' Who do you really want to be and what sort of legacy do you really want to leave?"

That's an incredibly important question for all of us.

In leadership, "It if ain't broke, don't fix it" is the very recipe for death. Complacency, the inability to adapt and change and refocus based on a reframe leads to a death spiral.

You have probably heard of the famous sigmoid curve.[1] If not, here is a visual:

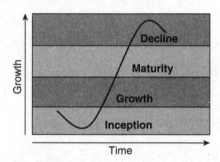

While the curve is in reality a mathematical model, the business thinker and writer Charles Handy applied it to organization leadership. It works like this...

Most organizations think that they need to change things, to innovate, when they bottom out, when sales drop, or competitors move in, or morale plummets. But by then, honestly, it is usually too late.

In reality, the time to refocus and innovate is at the height of your success, because that is when you have the most energy and resources to do so. It involves reinventing yourself before you have to. All of the great companies in history have done this. And formerly great companies that do not do this are no longer great.

Today the speed of the curves is increasing! The time to create the second curve of innovation and change is before the first curve has peaked, before most people even see any need to change.

Now, listen, we know this is hard work! There's nothing easy about driving change when things are going well, when people are happy if not complacent, and when the bottom line looks good. But this is part of the work of leadership.

When we are successful we tend to become myopic. We tend to only see things that confirm what we already believe. And that means we are unintentionally thwarting the very things that could propel us successfully into the future.

Tod Bolsinger did just this, changing both his personal leadership style and the organization's leadership structure. He was faced with resistance from some who said, "Why are you messing with something that is going so well?" Some even walked away. He lost beloved, long-time staff members. But the end result was an organization with renewed vitality and health, because he had dared to Refocus.

What in your life or organization needs to change—right now—before it even has to? With whom can you brainstorm the possibilities?

Part of Gage's problem is that he has a bunch of people around him who know he is "the brand" and who are not willing to say much, if anything, to challenge him. This is always dangerous, because it locks the leader into the way she has always thought and keeps everyone else content with the status quo. Under that set of circumstances, it becomes impossible to execute the last of our three activities—Reimagine.

Reframing helps us see the past differently. Refocusing allows us to think differently about today. Reimagining allows us to create a legacy for the future.

One of the most influential rock bands in the world over the last several decades has been Ireland's U2. Other groups are younger and hipper, but none are more influential. At the height of their success, they declared, "We have to go away and dream it up all over again." Instead of continuing to churn out chart-topping singles, they took a hiatus for creative and restorative purposes, to consider their mission and purpose as a band. Many years later, their success continues.

Such reimagining is essential for organizations as well. In his best-selling book, *Being Mortal: Medicine and What Matters Most in the End* (Metropolitan Books, 2014), Atul Gawande gives a wonderful example of reframing, refocusing, and reimagining. He tells the story of Dr. Bill

Thomas, a Harvard Medical School graduate who eventually ended up leading the Chase Memorial Nursing Home. Dr. Thomas spent most of his adult life becoming increasingly self-sufficient, which is what he believed was the pinnacle of human existence. He lived on a farm, grew most of his own vegetables, and used solar and wind power for electricity. While many of his Harvard colleagues were making gazillions of dollars in prestigious hospitals, Thomas chose a simpler path. To complement and support his lifestyle, he took a "day job" with regular hours at Chase.

But what he encountered at Chase was the exact opposite of self-sufficiency. He encountered despair, depression, and hopelessness in the residents. His initial "frame" on the situation was a medical frame. He had all of the residents evaluated. He examined prescriptions. After an extended period of medical evaluations, and frustrated staff, he realized that he had the wrong frame. His Harvard education gave him the first interpretation and solution: treatment. But, as he got to know the situation, he was able to reframe the problem. The problem was not medical, it was emotional. And the emotional problems were threefold: boredom, loneliness, and helplessness, according to Gawande.

If the problem was not medical, the solution was not going to be treatment. The solution needed to be "life." As he looked around the facility, he noticed that everything was sterile, medical, and plastic.

Once he had reframed the problem, he was able to refocus and reimagine new solutions. The nursing home applied for an innovation grant, and received it. They used the grant to create life at Chase. They brought dogs and cats to the nursing home. They replaced plastic greenery with real plants and flowers. A vegetable garden was planted. Staff brought their children in after school. While regulations did not allow it, they even received an exemption to bring in 100 birds. The reasoning? In the three or four winter months, the only sounds in the nursing home were moans, televisions, and electronic beeps. They wanted to create birdsong! Life was created at Chase Memorial Nursing Home.

How? Because Bill Thomas reframed, refocused, and reimagined.

President Thomas Jefferson never in his life ventured more than 50 miles from his home (can you imagine?). Yet he had a vision for the westward expansion of the United States. When he built Monticello, he built it to face West. He saw clearly—he IMAGINED clearly—what America could become.

And he inspired two men to go westward. Two guys named Meriwether Lewis and William Clark. Their westward venture—supported and initiated by Jefferson—led to the Louisiana Purchase, which doubled the size of the United States, all because Jefferson had reimagined what American could and should be. Tod Bolsinger unpacks this inspiring story, as it applies to leadership, in *Canoeing the Mountains.*

Jefferson lived in the same way as did the ancient father of the Hebrew nation who planted a tamarisk tree. This is one of slowest growing trees. It becomes majestic over time, but not in the lifetime of the one who planted it.

Why would one do such a thing?

Because of imagination. Because of a deep desire to leave a legacy. Remember, we all have a desire to belong, to contribute, and to make a difference. For Gage, it took a look inside to discover what he had lost. And none of us are exempt. It is only when we are willing to confront our deepest fears that we can reframe, refocus, and reimagine.

If you had to "go away and dream it all up again" for your life or organization, what would be the fulfillment of that dream? It is not just a hypothetical question. We believe that if you do this, you will be well on your way to discovering your secret sauce.

7
LETTING IT ALL GO

Two years later, Gage was back at the country club again. The scene was much different. No more gray winter skies. This time, Gage took in the smell of fresh-cut grass. It was May and the golf course was finally open for the season. Gage was still processing that earlier conversation as if it were yesterday. He was still pondering the question: Who do you need to be, Gage? But for the first time in many years, he felt like a new man. He spent at least 25 hours a week in the kitchen. No more tequila. The sleepless nights were few and far between. He had even written a letter to his Dad, expressing his anger . . . as well as his forgiveness. Of course, he had no way of sending it to his Dad, because he didn't know where he was.

But this time, Gage was truly back for the golf. He was ready for some fun. He spent 30 minutes at the range with Chip, and then played the back nine with a member.

That night Gage and Chip had dinner in a small, yet exquisite local restaurant, The Mountain Bistro. They dined on the local specialty—locally caught trout from the streams in Valle Crucis. Even international food star Gage was impressed!

"Man, all of the stuff I have heard about the food culture in North Carolina is true, Chip!" Gage exclaimed as he polished off his blackberry cobbler. "I have to feature this area on my show. Those fried green tomatoes were amazing!"

"Glad you enjoyed it, Gage. And I hope you liked our house wine . . . sweet tea!" Chip said with a smile.

For a few minutes, the two men talked about Gage's business as the talk drifted away from food and golf. A decade earlier, Gage had risen to food celebrity prominence by dint of his lovingly crafted homemade mole sauce, which had created a minor sensation as foodies made pilgrimages to sample it and purchased hundreds of thousands of the bottled sauce. At the time, there was nothing hotter than mole.

But over the years, sales of the sauce had tailed off. Gage still believed it to be delicious, but he realized something had to change. His advisers offered a number of explanations. The public's tasted had changed, some said. Others had copied his mole sauce and had undercut his price point, some argued. As Gage studied the issue, he came to believe that the main reason was that his bottled sauce used a lot of preservatives and contained a fair amount of processed sugar. People these days were into organic foods and very cautious about genetically modified offerings on their menu.

No doubt, Gage's sauce still tasted great, but he had become convinced that his ingredients and manufacturing process were simply out of step.

Gage had taken his proposals to his executives and Board. A few got it. Some—maybe most—thought he was nuts. After all, this delicious mole sauce had propelled the company and restaurant chain to great heights and had even made a few people quite rich. "This would be like Colonel Sanders changing the chicken recipe!" exclaimed one incredulous board member.

At first, Gage had tried gentle persuasion, but as the internal resistance grew he found himself lapsing into the impatience and the bull-in-a-china-shop management practices of his early career. He knew where the company needed to go—he just wasn't sure exactly how to get there or how to bring others along as he went.

He expressed his frustration to Chip and was taken aback by Chip's short answer. "I actually think it's a fairly simple solution, Gage."

Chip continued. "Look, you have done an amazing job over the last few years of creating alignment in your company. People are on board and excited about your mission, values, and strategy. You've been profitable and you are no longer just a renegade if talented chef. You've become a leader. You've rediscovered your passion. You've started answering the question about who you need to be. I'm proud of you, Gage.

"But now may be the time for you and your team to unlearn everything you have learned over the last decade!"

Gage was even further taken aback when Chip switched the conversation suddenly to golf.

"So, Gage, how did you feel about our time on the range today?"

Gage decided to go with the flow and get back to business later.

"Chip, it was great. I felt like it made a big difference to me. And here's the thing. I am eager to pair your insights with all the stuff I have been getting from watching the Golf Channel. I love to watch their show Morning Drive *while I am working out in the morning. I love that host Gary Williams. Didn't he used to have a radio show in Charlotte, here in North Carolina? Anyway, I am an aficionado.*

"And I am learning a lot from the Golf Channel and I am even subscribing to Golf Digest *now. I am trying to get the important stuff down, the stuff I am reading."*

Chip said nothing, so Gage continued.

"Here, let me look." Gage pulled out his iPhone and called up the Notes app.

"The main things I am focusing on right now are to turn my hips, start with my feet, and keep my left arm straight. These are the golden tips, aren't they, doc?"

Chip smiled. "Gage, there is some wisdom in each of those tips. At least a little bit. But none of them are going to ensure a good golf swing or a good golf game for you.

"As a matter of fact, I am going to give you my very best tip of all."

Gage was all ears. The "very best tip" from this legendary teaching professional?

"Chip, I'm all in. What is it?"

Chip smiled and sat back in his chair, as if he had all the time in the world.

"Forget absolutely everything you have ever heard about the golf swing, Gage."

Gage was dumbfounded. "Forget everything? Do you remember how bad I was when I came to see you ten years ago? I thought you would be impressed that I was working to get better!"

"Gage, I have always been impressed with you, my friend. By your passion and your acumen both. But I want you to forget all the noise in your

head when it comes to the golf swing. It's too much stuff. There is no way you can swing the club well when your head is full of thoughts about your feet, your arms, and your hips! It's too much noise!"

"I am assuming you still hold to a good posture and grip. Now, I simply want you to think about two things, as a right-handed golfer.

"I want you to swing with your right arm, as if you are skipping a rock across a pond.

"And I want you to keep the club pressed gently against your right index finger.

"Skip a rock and gently press the club, both with your right hand and arm. And when you warm up, don't use your left arm at all. Swing with your right arm.

"That's it. Forget everything else. Forget your feet, your hips, your shoulders. Forget swinging down on the ball. Forget inside out. Not that those things aren't correct, it's just too much to think about. Keep your club pressed against your right index finger and the rest will follow."

Gage was utterly befuddled.

"Chip, that is something a five-year-old kid could do! There is no way the golf swing is anywhere near that simple! I mean, come on!"

For the first time in their relationship, Gage actually doubted Chip a bit. He was all for simplicity, he reasoned, but this was downright ridiculous! Surely the golf swing could not be this simple. To say he was surprised would be an understatement.

He recalled all of the information on the Internet, TV, and in golf magazines about stacked swings, and torque, and plane and all manner of complicated things. He had bought every swing tool imaginable. One club would break apart if swung incorrectly. Another club forced his arms and hands into the perfect triangle for putting. Golf experts critiqued his video analysis, when he uploaded his swing to the Internet. For Gage, the golf swing had become like physics, complicated beyond measure and so seductively interesting. There was simply no way it could be reduced to skipping rocks across a pond and pressing one finger lightly.

But Chip had never led Gage astray before and, after a bit of reflection Gage saw Chip's insight for what it was: a message that he had to unlearn everything he thought he knew.

IT'S ALL IN THE SYSTEM

As we explained in chapter 5, creating a culture of engagement—one where people belong, contribute, and make a difference—requires core alignment. But this is easier said than done. How many of us have sat in meetings where a facilitator leads us in a kum-bah-yah session of writing core values or mission statements. After the bonfire is over, we return to our jobs and nothing has changed. In fact, we often become even more cynical after those sessions because we realize how worthless they truly are! We throw those exercises into the same category as "trust falls" and "ropes courses," all nice experiences, but nothing that really sticks.

What makes core alignment so difficult is that, by definition, it is an ongoing process of change. To be effective, it must result in a change to the culture. But all human systems tend to maintain the status quo. Think about your own family, as an example. Which family dysfunctions have been passed on from generation to generation? Remember Xerox, the golden child of most business schools in the 1970s? Corporate inertia blinded them from rising competition until it was too late. Look at how many historical downtown churches have closed down in recent years. Changing demographics in the community have nudged many churches into irrelevance.

If there is one thing we have learned over years of working with all organizations, it is this: systems have power. All human systems fight to preserve the status quo, even if that results in death!

Like fish in water, we live in systems often unaware of how they shape us. But everything is connected.

Human beings live and move in systems; life is a dynamic interplay between people and events. And the systems we live in produce certain predictable results. This is true for your personal life and the life of your organization.

In our thinking about systems we draw on the work of writers like Peter Senge and Ronald Heifetz and on disciplines such as family therapy. We believe that systems thinking is a way of seeing and understanding the world that takes into account the fact that humans are highly complex and relational creatures.

The world is not created of separate and unrelated forces. Everything meshes. However, as individuals we have difficulty seeing the whole pattern.

Systems thinking is a conceptual framework, a body of knowledge and tools that has been developed over the last half-century to make the full pattern clearer and to help us see how to change things effectively and with the least amount of effort.

It is all about finding leverage points—and this is true in our lives and in our organizations. Thinking wisely and well and systemically is a game changer.

More often than we realize, systems cause their own crises. That is hard for us to see, because we tend to blame external forces or the mistakes of individuals. We look for scapegoats. We blame others. We sometimes blame ourselves. But, in fact, we are all caught up in a complex interworking of dynamics that shape our behavior more than we would care to admit.

Here are some basic facts, from Senge's work in *The Fifth Discipline*, about how we are shaped by systems:

- Today's problems come from yesterday's "solutions." What worked in the past does not work anymore because of a change in the competitive landscape.
- The harder you push, the harder the system pushes back. The system is an unforgiving thing. It cannot be defeated, only understood and, over time, transformed.

- Faster often results in slower. It is difficult to overestimate the importance of critical reflection and of building ownership of stakeholders on the front end of a change initiative.
- Small changes can produce big results—but the areas of greatest leverage are often the least obvious.
- There is no one to blame. We tend to want to make people scapegoats and culprits. But in fact people generally behave exactly how the system rewards them for behaving.

What do all of these facts have in common? They are counterintuitive.

There is nothing easy or obvious about forging a great corporate culture. It requires disrupting the status quo, or the balance of things with which we have become so comfortable.

According to Heifetz, you know you are dealing with a systemic issue if you have...

- a cycle of failure,
- an overdependence on authority,
- an increasing number of complaints,
- tried to solve the same problem with the same people multiple times,
- increased levels of conflict.

The status quo is a tenacious thing! Over time, the structures and defaults that make up an organizational system become deeply ingrained and very hard to reshape. There is a self-reinforcing nature to the "way we have always done things around here."

Often our worse enemy is our past success. We get trapped into doing things that have always worked in the past, even if those once-valid approaches are not the most effective anymore.

We all have default ways of behaving, thinking, and leading. Our "defaults" are comfortable for us largely because they have worked in the past. But the downside of defaults is that they blind us to a more robust and wider array of solutions that could actually create more value.

We want to belong, contribute, and make a difference. None of that comes easily or naturally. To create a great culture, we have to disrupt the status quo. There are two types of disruptions: external and internal.

EXTERNAL DISRUPTIONS

Recently, we consulted with a general store in Nebraska. The store sold meats, vegetables, dairy products, clothing, hardware, toys, candy, music, and everything else you might imagine from a general store. They even had a computer repair service and tanning beds. Talk about the need to do a few things well!

We were brought in due to a seismic shift in this small town. Walmart had just announced plans to build a new mega store, less than a mile away. Before we ever arrived, the third-generation owners knew they had to change or die. Their options? Relocate. Create a niche. Win on personalized service.

But they knew they could not compete head to head with Walmart on volume or price. What to do? What would you do?

Today, our world is in the midst of several seismic shifts. Andy Grove, founder and past Chairman of Intel, describes these shifts as "strategic inflection points." In a keynote speech he gave to the Academy of Management in 1998, he defines strategic inflection points as "what happens to a business when a major change takes place in its competitive environment. A major change due to introduction of new technologies. A major change due to the introduction of a different regulatory environment. The major change can be simply a change in the customers' values, a change in what customers prefer. . . . What is common to all of them and what is key is that they require a fundamental change in business strategy, and that's almost a definition of a

Strategic Inflection Point. A Strategic Inflection Point is that which causes you to make a fundamental change in business strategy. Nothing less is sufficient.

These strategic inflection points, or external disruptions, regardless of your industry come from a handful of sources:

- *Changing Technologies.* Consider the rapid pace of change in this arena and whether or not your organization has kept up. When external change outpaces internal change, organizational struggle is inevitable. Think Blockbuster. Now think video-on-demand on virtually every device you own.

- *Changing Demographics.* Currently, the population of the United States sits at around 300 million. By the middle of the twenty-first century, the US population will grow to roughly 440 million. Most of that increase will be driven by immigration. One in five Americans will be foreign born by 2050. Currently, 13 percent of the population is age 65 or older. That will increase to 20 percent by 2050.

- *Changing Regulations.* As the world changes, we can expect to see consistent regulatory changes to every industry. Consider the impact of deregulation in the banking industry in 1980 and how that led to banks operating across state lines, the blurring of services where insurance companies became banks and banks became insurance companies. The resulting competition created consumer benefits, such as lower interest rates, but also contributed to the Great Recession. Regulations will always have unintended consequences, and the impact could be a strategic reflection point.

- *Changing Consumer Appetites.* Consumers are fickle. One day, Americans indulge in carbohydrates and shunning beef. The next, we are eating beef and shedding carbs. Trends in the markets for clothing, toys, collectibles, and entertainment are constantly causing changes in the demand for these products as well. Consider the ever-changing landscape of popular music. From guitar-driven 1970s rock, to synthetic 1980s pop, to organic grunge in the 1990s, back to syrupy-sweet boy bands and pretty little starlets in the 2000s and beyond. Sure, some have staying power. But in general, consumer appetites follow trends and fads. Fads are not necessarily external disruptions, unless they completely change an industry.

- *Changing Economics.* Think about how your grandparents or great-grandparents changed their behavior, even the course of their lives, based on their experience of the Great Depression. A generation of frugal savers emerged. People were risk averse. Several decades later, Americans rode prosperity to the brink in the dot-com era. Housing prices surged. Net wealth, at least on paper, was immense. Risk aversion gave way to betting on the next big thing. And then the American economy was rocked again. Lehman Brothers. AIG. Bank of America and Countryside. We all felt the reverberations through our 401ks and savings accounts. Once again, we experienced a major external disruption that impacted every American industry.

- *Changing Media.* Civilization has evolved through four strategic inflection points related to communications: oral, print, broadcast, and digital. Each of these primary media has radically changed human behavior, socialization, and institutions. What is next?

Each of the above trends is a potential source of external disruption. They force us to function differently. Our choice is simple: change or die.

There is hardly any business, any organization in the world that has not been impacted in one way or another by the enormous changes of the past few years—changes brought about by the global economy, by the changing culture, by changing tastes in the marketplace, by technological change, by the digital era.

Some organizations live on the razor edge of change, constantly upgrading, retooling, retrenching, reinvesting, reinventing—and these are the organizations that become the leaders in their corner of the marketplace.

And then there are those organizations that resist change. When the next wave comes, they drown, they disappear. Change is inevitable—but keeping up with change is not. That takes work and awareness. The organizations that are the most likely to make a healthy transition through times of external or internal change are those that have a dynamic culture, one where people have the opportunity to belong, contribute, and make a difference.

This kind of organization tends to be more flexible and responsive to new situations, less set in its ways. An organization's ability to adapt and respond to change can spell the difference between success and extinction.

Have you ever heard the adjective "Chaplinesque"? It means, "in the style of Charlie Chaplin." The very last thing you would want to be known as during changing times is "Chaplinesque." Charlie Chaplin was a comic film star during the era of silent movies. His world abruptly changed with the 1927 release of *The Jazz Singer*, the first "talking picture." Chaplin was slow to grasp the meaning of adding sound to motion pictures. In 1931, he predicted that the "fad" of talking pictures would soon pass away. "I give the talkies six months more," he said.

Question: When was the last time you saw a silent movie?

In today's environment, organizations must stay on top of changing conditions. They must be fluid and constantly changing, because conditions are fluid and constantly changing. People come and go, move out of old roles and into new ones. Conditions change. New technologies emerge. New laws and regulations are promulgated. Economic and market conditions fluctuate. In a rapidly evolving world, organizations with dynamic cultures navigate change with alacrity and agility, while clinging firmly to their core principles.

Those organizations that do not manage change are doomed to be managed by it—if not flattened by it. Those that manage change well are the innovators and leaders in society.

Change is inevitable in life and in business. The rate of change is undeniably accelerating. Whereas previous generations only had to deal with gradual change in life and in business, today's generations must deal with bewildering, quantum-leap change, or external disruptions.

Another example of an external disruption comes from the communications arena: for thousands of years, books were made by hand-copying manuscripts. In the 1439, Johannes Gutenberg made the printing press possible by inventing movable type. In 1885–480 years after Gutenberg—Ottmar Mergenthaler introduced the Linotype "hot lead" typesetter, which mechanized typesetting by setting "slugs" of type from a typewriter-like keyboard.

Phototypesetting was born in the 1940s with a primitive machine called the Intertype Fotosetter, but it was not until the photo imaging "back end" was married to the computer display "front end" that computerized phototypesetting became widespread in the 1970s. Even so, the job of a Linotype operator was very secure from the 1880s to the 1970s, when rapid sales of computerized phototypesetters ("cold type") edged the Linotype ("hot type") aside.

The job security of cold type operators was extremely short lived by comparison: by the late 1980s, when desktop publishing made almost every computer owner a typesetter and graphic designer, the specialized career of "typesetter" was gone forever. All previous changes had been gradual—but computers and desktop publishing represented an external disruption in the publishing and typesetting arena.

Leaders in organizations must learn to lead through times of rapid change. They must pay attention to external disruptions, and learn to discern which of these are mere passing fads and which are likely to force quantum change upon the organization. The rise of new competitors, the rise of new technologies, the obsolescence of old technologies, changes in global conditions and foreign economies, changes in government regulations (including deregulation), changing customer demographics and tastes—all of these factors have the potential of imposing external disruption on your organization.

How, then, does a leader lead through times of enormous external and internal change? Here are some suggestions:

1. Be aware and be proactive. Make sure you stay up on trends and changes in, and influences on your organization's environment. Read, study, talk to experts, enlist the services of consultants, find out what people are saying, thinking, and doing in your industry.

Beware of becoming isolated or insulated within the ivory tower of your corner office. Be informed about opportunities before they become *missed* opportunities. A reporter once asked Wayne Gretzky why he was such a great hockey player, to which Gretzky replied, "I skate where the puck is going to be."[1] Identify where your "puck" is going to be, and proactively lead your organization there.

2. Listen to your intuition. There is nothing mystical about intuition. It is the ability of our brains to sift through mountains of input, experience, memories, and events at a subconscious level and, out of all of that input, produce a decision or an idea. Sometimes we can perform all the studies, examine all the graphs and charts, analyze all the data, and listen to all the consultants and focus groups, yet still come up with a sense that "I've got to go with my gut on this one." That's intuition. Visionary leaders are those who have learned to tune in to their intuition, even when it saws across the grain of logic, in order to take advantage of opportunities before they would normally present themselves to the logical, "sensible" mind. The ability to intuit is a priceless ability. Cultivate it.

3. Listen to organizational dissonance. In times of external disruption, there is often a difference, a dissonance, between what an organization says and what it does. Executives, CEOs, managers, pastors, and board members may be charting one course, while the people on the front lines are moving in a different direction. Who is right? Who is out of step with reality? Who is responding to change? Who is resisting change?

Never assume that the senior leadership has all the answers. Sometimes the people "at the top" are isolated and out of touch, while the people in the trenches have a better feel for what is going on—but not always. Sometimes the leadership is on the cutting edge, while the front line troops just do not want to deal with change. As a leader, when you encounter dissonance in your organization, it is up to you to sift through the dissonance and find out where the truth lies.

4. *Pay attention to your No. 1 competitor.* Why is your competitor doing so well? What is your competitor doing that you are not—and vice versa? How is your competitor responding to changing conditions both outside and inside the organization? What does your competitor see that you might be missing?

5. *Listen to your people.* The people on the front lines of your organization are closest to potential external disruptions. Whether employees, team members, or volunteers, encourage them to be observant and ask them about the changes in the environment of your organization. Wander around and ask your people what they observe. Suggestion boxes or reports rarely work because they are anonymous and not relational. Include as many people as possible in your visioning process. Employees want to be heard—and they want immediate feedback. In fact, this is part of empowering them to belong, contribute, and make a difference.

But external disruptions are far easier to manage than internal disruptions.

INTERNAL DISRUPTIONS

It is entirely possible that David Marsh is the greatest coach in any sport, ever.

Does that sound over the top?

If so, check out his resume. As the swimming coach (men's and women's) at Auburn University, Marsh won 12 national championships. He is an eight-time national coach of the year.

After the 2007 season, he accepted an offer to be the Head Elite Coach and CEO of the US Olympic Committee Center of Excellence with SwimMAC Carolina. At the time of the writing if this book, he has led SwimMAC to three consecutive USA club excellence championships, a first for any program, outdistancing the second-place finisher by 12,000 points. He has coached 47 Olympians.

Simply put, no coach in any sport has ever matched this record of success.

We have been privileged to get to know him personally. (In fact, one of our daughters swims at SwimMAC.) Today, he is at the peak of his profession. But he was not when he started at Auburn.

When he took over the program in 1990 at the age of 30, the team had scored no points in the previous years' Southeastern Conference championship meet. It is tough to do that.

When he interviewed for the job, Marsh told the Auburn athletic director (and legendary football coach), Pat Dye, that his aspirations went beyond college to the Olympics. But Auburn did not seem to be a fertile place for such ambition.

"I was determined that we were going to be a championship program," Marsh told us. "At first, we didn't have the athletes for that. But if nothing else, they could look like champions."

At the first practice Marsh led, his team never got into the water.

"I noticed they did not do a good job of greeting alumni. So we worked on how to shake hands well and look people in the eye. We taught them how to place the towel around their neck and to have a posture that looked like Superman. We taught them to act "AS IF" they were champions even before they were.

"It started with how they behaved and how they looked. They were going to act like champions, from the very first day."

Early on, Coach Marsh was put to the test. After the team had competed well in the SEC meet for the first time in a long time, the swimmers celebrated by going to a beer party in a dorm, something strictly against regulations. Marsh confirmed that this was the case, and acted quickly.

He kicked every member off of the team!

He had an assistant convey the bad news, saying, "If you want to have any chance of being back on the team, you must make an appointment and talk to Coach Marsh personally."

The assistant reported that many of the swimmers were crying, to which Marsh replied "Good!"

This was a radical disruption of the status quo and one that came at personal risk to Marsh. After all, you do not kick your whole team off of the team! But Marsh had keen insight that the system of the Auburn swim program was broken and the only way out was to be disruptive.

You get them to look people in the eyes, shake hands, drape the towel around the neck like a champion, aspire to Superman in posture and, when the values are violated, kick everyone off of the team.

You do not let the swimmers get into the water at their first practice.

That is how you are a positively disruptive force.

Since coming to Charlotte, Marsh has continued to be a disruptive force. For generations, the assumption has been that swimmers needed endless hours of grueling training in the pool. Marsh has stood this conventional wisdom on its head, instituting much shorter workouts focused on speed and technique. This was a true innovation in the discipline of swim coaching.

Such counterintuitive methods have inspired world-class athletes like Olympians Ryan Lochte and Cullen Jones to relocate to Charlotte, which prior to Marsh had little tradition of world-class swimming. Along with Ryan and Cullen, many members of SwimMAC's "Team Elite" believe their best bet to win gold at the Olympics is by working under this disruptive, iconoclastic coach.

Throughout his storied career, David Marsh has had this as a slogan: "A Culture of Excellence Is a Culture of Struggle."

We could not say it better. A culture of excellence is a culture of struggle. External disruptions are easier, because we have no choice. Internal disruptions are much more difficult. Whether you are turning around a losing swim program, revitalizing a dying church, or transitioning from a top-down leadership model to a collaborative culture, internal disruptions face resistance.

The old adage says, "If it ain't broke don't fix it." That is a convenient slogan to use to avoid the difficult process of change. But the best time to initiate internal disruption is when things are going well, when you have the resources and assets to leverage in a new way. Let us look at ten lessons learned from Coach Marsh, when leading internal disruption:

1. Start with a simple change, but it must be a change related to values, behaviors, or attitudes. Note that Coach Marsh started with an attitude change, but it was simple. "We worked on how to shake hands well and look people in the eye. We taught them how to place the towel around their neck and to have a posture that looked like Superman. We taught them to act 'AS IF' they were champions even before they were."

2. Find solutions that challenge the prevailing power structure. The prevailing structure at Auburn was one that exists in many college and professional sports programs: athletes call the shots. Without athletes, you do not have a team. So what did Marsh do? He kicked everyone off the team!

3. Make sure your rules have teeth. Marsh was willing to take an enormous risk. He put his own job on the line when he dismissed the entire team. But without teeth, there will be no internal disruption.

4. Experiment and take smart risks. Over the years, Marsh has experimented and tinkered with and challenged conventional wisdom.

5. Fix the system, not the person. While Coach Marsh will address behavioral issues in the program, if required, he does so to reinforce values. His individual focus, however, is much more on development

and encouragement. At SwimMAC, as at Auburn, his "fixes" tend to be systemic, rather than individualized. He has learned that you do not create a policy to deal with one person's problems. When you do that, the solution becomes the problem.

6. Do not rely on controls. Increase accountability, and decrease bureaucracy. Accountability is organic and leads to alignment. It includes elements of both encouragement and correction, but it is not punitive. It reinforces values. Bureaucracy addresses behaviors and actions, but allows little room for judgment and is often out of sync with values. Coach Marsh has created cultures of high accountability and low bureaucracy.

7. Do not build systems to change behavior. Instead, build systems that attract the right people and eject the wrong people. Over time, Marsh created a world-class program at Auburn. But it was not due to luck. He took the same approach when he took over SwimMAC in Charlotte. He is currently attracting many of the best and most talented swimmers in the country.

8. Find your own solutions. Do not copy others. Too often, when leading internal disruption, leaders look externally for solutions. But the real answers are always organic. They are discovered from within. Marsh is redefining a sport, but is doing so from the ground up. While he is an avid learner, he has recognized that change starts from the inside out.

9. Prepare for struggle. Marsh understands that internal disruption takes trial and error. Failure is a part of the game. In fact, everything we have learned about Coach Marsh suggests that he values a culture of excellence over a culture of winning. Wins will come as a byproduct of a great culture. He told us he would rather see a young swimmer lose the race, swimming with great technique, than win a race, while swimming like a water bug. Marsh has proven that a great culture is a successful culture. But there are no easy answers or quick fixes. A culture of excellence comes from a culture of struggle.

Change is rarely pleasant and never easy, but the ability to safely navigate change is one of the crucial vital signs of a great culture. If people do not feel like they can contribute, change will be impossible. You will not have their buy-in. If they do not feel like they belong, they will not embrace change. If they do not feel like they are making a difference, they will not support the changes necessary to align with the core ideology. A static organization is headed for extinction, if it is not dead already. But the ability to adapt and respond to change is the key to success and a bright future. To create alignment, disruption is necessary. But neither alignment nor disruption is the secret sauce. Are you ready to find out what really is the secret sauce? Turn the page.

8

WHAT'S THE SECRET SAUCE?

Gage had returned home, but his conversation with Chip stayed with him daily.

It had been a shock to his system to consider that he and his team needed to forget everything they had learned in the past ten years if they were to continue to be successful and to meet new challenges. Gage had been dead set against moving ahead with what had worked in the past, but he was coming to understand that disrupting the status quo was the only way that his business would move forward without stagnating.

He was committed to his decision to make the ingredients in his sauce more organic and healthy, to cut out preservatives as much as possible even though that would increase his manufacturing costs. What he needed to figure out how to do now was to bring his team along with him.

And he had realized something else as well. His disruption of the status quo was not simply a technical, manufacturing issue. It would require a change in the culture of his company as well. In the early days, they had been about living large, building a "caliente company," premium given to taste and boldness, with little to no thought given to health and self-care.

The product was so good and the marketing so clever that they had built a mini-empire. But as Gage aged he came to realize that his own life was not sustainable if he continued eating and living the way he had been. Sure, he had quit the tequila shots and had worked through some personal issues. And he was feeling a growing responsibility to care for the health and well-being of his customers. He was moving from caring for himself to caring for others.

His company would have to undergo a culture shift where it went from all taste all the time to great taste as a part of healthy choices. His own evolution mirrored that in the culture as a whole, so it was good for business.

But beyond that, Gage felt that it was the right thing to do.

There was one problem. Gage had no idea how in the world to lead in such a way that the culture of his company shifted in this new, disruptive direction. He saw what had to happen—saw the future—clear as day. But, how to get there . . . ?

He drew upon the help of several business consultants, but that only confused matters.

One said that he needed to take a "damn the torpedoes" style. "You're the founder, you're the brand, you're the future. No one can see the future except you. You need to be 'Chainsaw Gage.' Tell people to get on or get off the bus."

Another consultant said, "Your job as a leader is to get consensus. You can't make a cultural change like this unless everyone is on board. The one mistake you could make would be to go too fast and leave anyone behind."

A third consultant weighed in. "Look, you're worrying too much about the human element in this deal. It's an economic decision and a technical manufacturing decision. Frame it up that way. People can't argue with reason and, if they do, they are probably not the right people for you anyway."

Gage saw grains of truth in each piece of feedback, but found none satisfying or resonant with the man and leader he was becoming. So he brooded and puzzled.

Until one day, he was hit with a flash of insight. He was on the practice green at his local golf course, working on pitching and putting, when the thought came to him.

"The best consultant I have ever had is Chip, and he's not even a consultant! That guy gets way more than golf. He seems to get life and leadership too."

Fueled with a new sense of hope, Gage hopped on the first flight he could find heading East to North Carolina and showed up unannounced. When he got to the club, he went straight to the practice range and caught Chip's eye. The golf pro looked up in surprise, and his expression quickly changed to concern. Giving his student a break, Chip strode over to Gage.

"Gage, I am surprised to see you. Is everything alright? We don't have an appointment, do we? Oh, but by the way, it is great to see you!"

Gage patted the air with his hands. "No, no, Chip, everything is fine! I just needed to ask you something and wanted to do it in person. Do you have any time?"

Thought lines creased Chip's forehead. "I would love to spend time with you, but we have a charity event today and then I have an early morning flight out of Charlotte for a seminar in Florida. I have about one hour free this afternoon, around 5 o'clock. Could we talk then?"

Gage was grateful for anything and quickly agreed.

At the appointed time, Gage showed up at the range, seven iron in hand. Early in their relationship, Chip had given Gage the advice of the legendary Texas golf pro Harvey Penick: "Pick one club and learn to love it like a girlfriend." Gage had chosen the seven iron, a versatile club, and it had served him well. He thought he would double up on their time together by having Chip watch him hit a few shots.

As he hit a few shots to the target green, Gage outlined both his current dilemma and his thoughts on a consulting relationship to Chip. Three perfect shots in a row nearly hit the flag. But then he shanked a ball that sprayed wide right, nearly hitting a golf cart heading up the path. After feeling his face turn red, he quickly hit two more shanks. His nerves had taken over. He wanted to hire Chip as a management consultant, and the initial retainer, as well as the hourly rate he offered, would have been eye popping to most people. Within a couple years, Chip would be set for life. Gage would cover all of Chip's expenses, and he would provide Chip with access to his private jet, part of a fractional ownership that Gage had bought into a year earlier. But he wasn't sure how Chip was going to respond. His last three shots exposed his nerves.

It would have been a most attractive offer to any consulting professional, and Gage finished his pitch with a flourish. "So, what about it Chip? Will you come along with us and change the food world in the same way you are changing the golf world?"

Chip smiled at his friend. "Gage, I am honored you would ask me to do this. It is very meaningful to me. And the money is staggering. But, my calling is to be a club professional...

"Listen. I would be honored to continue to serve you in any way I can. As a matter of fact, as the years have gone by I have noticed that we talk not only about golf but about life and business as well. Your offer tells me that we've both recognized this reality."

Gage nodded, still a little stunned that Chip could turn down his offer. In his world, very few people would turn down such a large sum!

Chip continued. "One of the things I have realized through the years, Gage, has been that every person seems to have this built-in need to experience what they were created to need. It really boils down to three things, I think. First, they need to belong to something or someone bigger than themselves. Second, they want to make a contribution, utilizing their unique gifts, skills, and talents. And finally, they want to make a difference in the world. No one wants to live a life that is meaningless, just footprints in the sand. Or should I say, footprints in the sand trap!

"You see, Gage, our relationship has been and continues to be a great gift to me. As I have been privileged to walk alongside you during your growing years as a leader, I have been able to clarify and better articulate my own core beliefs about life. It goes way beyond golf, and even beyond business. In all fairness, Gage, I should be paying YOU!

"As a matter of fact... Gage, I actually was going to call you about this, but wasn't sure exactly when...

"Well, I have come up with a name for what I believe to be my core belief, my central premise when it comes to leadership. I've been sharing this with my interns and staff to beta test the idea. And it is named in honor of you."

Gage dropped his jaw and his seven iron.

"You are kidding, Chip. After me?! If anything, I figured I would be your example of how NOT to do things!"

"Hear me out, Gage. You are becoming such a strong leader and you are moving into a part of your life where you have much to share with others. There's really only one thing I haven't shared with you.

"The Secret Sauce."

Gage laughed so loudly that he got dagger looks from a few of the older members on the practice range.

"Secret Sauce? What's that all about, Chip?"

Chip's smile crinkled his face. "Well, Gage, your claim to fame is your delicious mole sauce. But as you found out quickly, a great product won't build a great company. In the same way that a great strategy, great technology, great innovation, and even great people won't, in and of themselves, build a great organization.

"In recent years, a lot of people have got it right that organizational culture is all important. In my industry, many club professionals have started understanding this. At our last annual conference, the keynote speaker's presentation was all about "Great Club Cultures." But a ton of people have gotten stumped by the very thing that is stumping you right now—how do you GET that great culture? We can define culture, but how do you make it happen?"

"Chip, that's exactly it—it's where I am stuck. So, what's the answer? What's the Secret Sauce?"

Chip paused for a while. Then, his eyes twinkling, he spoke. "I think you're ready for the answer, Gage. But first, let's talk about golf. Just a few minutes ago, you hit three perfect shots, followed by three horrible shots. At this point, I'm more interested in how you recover from a bad shot, than how you swing the club... "

A CAUTIONARY TALE

A friend of ours turned around a 100-year-old organization in England several years ago. Let us call him Walter, and we will call the organization St. Michael's Academy. St. Michael's was almost dead when Walter took the reins. St. Michael's had a history of serving the children of affluence in one of the most prestigious corners of England. In recent years, however, the academy was in desperate need of renovation. Enrollment was down. And the last headmaster was fired after he was arrested for embezzling funds.

Walter had his hands full. But he instilled hope in his faculty and admin staff early on. He engaged them in a ten-year process of revamping the academy. Faculty had to take pay cuts during the early years. They sacrificed a great deal. They had to learn to collaborate and help teach in each other's classrooms. Walter challenged and confronted angry parents and alumni. He changed the admissions process dramatically. Wealth no longer dictated which students would be accepted. Students were accepted based on character, academics, and demonstrated service to the community. Faculty and staff had high levels of input and empowerment.

They were highly collaborative, trying new things and failing along the way. They worked in small groups. The staff ended up setting standards for how promotions and raises were awarded. Students started returning. At the end of ten years, Walter decided to package the product that his staff had built—a new model for education that he called "AcadeMIX." He exported it to the United States, found a publisher who put his book in a big-box store, and he started a speaking tour. Within a year, it was clear that AcadeMIX was a miserable failure in the United States. He never quite figured out why he was successful in England, but a flop in the United States.

Looking back, however, the answer is clear.

What made his effort successful was a ten-year quest for the Holy Grail, not finding the Grail. It was the quest itself. We could call it a journey, but a journey is simply moving from one place to another. This is more than a journey. We could call it an adventure. That is getting closer. But an adventure normally results in a return home. We set out into the unknown, on an adventure, but we eventually come home. A quest, however, involves a search for something. A ring. A Golden Fleece. Enlightenment. Whatever it is, it suggests that we will never return and we will never be the same. For St. Michael's, the quest was the answer. AcadeMIX was simply the product that was produced along the way. A throw-away souvenir. But AcadeMIX was not the secret sauce.

The quest created apostles. It created deep relationships. It allowed people to experiment and fail—and still feel okay about themselves. It gave faculty and staff alike a sense of ownership. The product was merely a byproduct.

This is true in creating culture. The content of a culture may be built around a product. But the quest to build a culture is the secret sauce. And that is not something that happens overnight.

As we work with clients—whether in leadership development, executive coaching, change leadership, or strategic planning—we emphasize that the quest, the process, is more important than the product, or the content.

Let us emphasize that: *The quest is more important than the product.*

The well-known writer and thinker Margaret Wheatley once told a group of TAG clients that "We can't know the future. But we can prepare for it by knowing ourselves."

It is all about the quest. It is all about the things that happen along the way.

And, now we are getting to the Secret Sauce.

Creating a great culture is not primarily about having a great idea, a great leader, a great product, a great sales force, great technology, or a great strategy.

It is about the quest.

To get a culture where people realize their innate desire to belong, contribute, and make a difference—that is the goal. The Secret Sauce is the process that engages people in creating their own culture. By creating the culture, they are creating something that they belong to, that they contribute to, and that makes a difference.

The Secret Sauce is not found in the culture itself. It is found in the quest that results in the culture. While everything that we have discussed in the book thus far is part of the quest, the Secret Sauce is the quest itself!

GETTING STARTED AS A CULTURE-SHAPER

Because you are reading this book, we assume you are a leader who is interested in seeing your organization live into a great culture. That is great. We are partners in the quest! Our great aspiration is to help you do that. None of us can do it alone.

As you began your quest as a culture-changer and culture-shaper, there are two initial things to keep in mind.

1. The first task of leadership is to distinguish between what needs to be preserved and what needs to change. As you work through changes in your organization, never lose sight of what must NOT change. Remember our discussion of core ideology—your organization's code and strategy. These should not shift with every wind of change. When you organization changes internally, or responds to important external changes, anything you do must be evaluated with a framework of protecting the organization's code while allowing the strategy to evolve.

2. When you come into an existing situation to make changes, be very careful not to condemn the past. Always frame your vision in a positive, upbeat way. Your job is not to erase the past, but to help the people envision a brighter future. The people you have come to lead have not failed in the past. Your job is to spur them on to greater heights in the future. These people were part of the past—they lived it, experienced it, were invested in it. If you condemn it, they will feel condemned as well. Always honor the past even as you are building the future. Even the most dysfunctional organization has some beautiful and worthy things in its past. Dwell on these, even as you chart the course to the future.

If you have led for any length of time, you know well that leadership is not about popularity. You may become a beloved leader one day, but if you are leading change and shaping a culture, there will be bumps along the way.

In their book *Leadership on the Line*, Ronald Heifetz and Marty Linsky said it well: "Leadership is disappointing people at a rate that they can tolerate."[1]

When we have shared this quote, younger leaders especially have given us a quizzical eye. After all, Google "leadership quotes" and you will get a multitude of inspiring statements about how leadership raises water levels, causes dangerous tides to recede, inspires millions, and, in general, is just about the best gosh-darned thing ever.

Experienced leaders, however, tell a different story. Especially those close to the ground and close to the people. Especially those who are involved in culture-changing and culture-shaping.

We are not reductionistic in our thinking. But we do want to be practical. We have decades of work invested with leaders and organizations in changing and shaping culture. We have worked with well-intentioned leaders who pushed through change initiatives, but never saw a cultural change. We have worked with talented leaders who could never quite grasp the dynamics that make up culture-shaping. What both groups lacked was that they never learned to lovingly and expertly cook the secret sauce.

With that in mind, we offer the Ten Commandments of Creating Culture. Think of these as the indispensable ingredients in the secret sauce.

TEN COMMANDMENTS OF CREATING A GREAT CULTURE

1. *Create Safe Places*. Our world is not safe. People look at the geopolitical situation, rising violence in many areas, both urban and rural, and a host of threats to their children, and they long for safety. Sadly, our organizations can often feel like the least safe place of all. Our churches are rife with division, our workplaces are full of petty politics and

backstabbing, our social and political institutions are seen as being populated by those who are "only in it for themselves" and can only seem to win election and promotion and position by dividing us rather than bringing us together. A leader who is leading change must ensure that his or her people feel safe. Safe to express their opinions, even when those opinions challenge the status quo. Safe to be themselves, to bring their gifts and talents to the table. Safe to face conflict and not just avoid it or survive it, but to thrive through it. In our experience, leaders often overestimate how safe their followers feel. The consequence of this is that these same leaders are often shocked when their people bail for another opportunity or actively work to undermine them when the opportunity presents itself. Ask yourself, leader, "Is this place a safe place?"

2. *Direct Intentional Conversations*. In the "old days," it was considered innovative to put a suggestion box in a common area where employees could vent privately and employers could quickly ignore said venting. A suggestion box may have been "safe," but it was not effective. Contrast that with recent tales from the corporate and political worlds where "whistleblowers" had their lives and careers ruined by daring to speak up. Every organization with a great culture has safe places where people can speak their minds, express their dissent, and call their leaders to account. Ask yourself, leader, "What specific and readily accessible forums have we created in our organization for people to speak their minds and hearts during this time of change?"

3. *Manage Anxiety Levels*. Anxiety is an unseen, internal fuel that drives us. It is entirely possible that we may be living in the time of the greatest anxiety in the history of the Western world. Anxiety is our natural response when we feel threatened or insecure. This threat always takes shape in our

minds and hearts as loss. "If I don't get up this morning and work hard, I will lose my job and have no money." "Even if I do get up this morning and work hard, I may lose my job and have no money." "I am never going to get ahead in this organization because these changes will take away my status, and all my years of investment will be for nothing." Know this, leader, if you are leading cultural change, there will be loss for some people, and when people feel the threat of loss, their anxiety goes through the roof. In our last chapter we will talk at length about how to manage your own anxiety as a leader and, rest assured, you are feeling it if you are engaged in the work of change leadership. The important thing for now is to realize that the people you are leading are feeling anxiety if you are engaged in the business of changing a culture, and to own the fact that you have the responsibility to create places for them to share this anxiety without being overwhelmed by it.

4. *Use the Water Cooler.* It is hard to describe the impact of "obeying" this command. Leaders who are managing change are, by definition, busy men and women. The good ones know that they must listen to their people so that they can understand, filter accurate information from people saying "what the boss wants to hear," and communicate personal care and concern for the team. So, there are a wide variety of recommendations offered for formal structures to accomplish this—e-mails sent directly to the leader, town hall meetings, focus groups where the boss reads the transcripts, "open door" policies during set office hours. There is nothing wrong with any of these, but none pack the power punch of tons of informal, off-the-clock, in the moment, unplanned conversations. Some of the very best leaders we have worked with schedule unscheduled time. Yep, you read that right. They build into their calendars time

for no formal meetings or phone calls or strategic planning.
They simply get out into the office or the field or the
congregation and talk to people. We think of the pastor of
a very large church who would routinely show up at Sunday
morning "huddles" where church volunteers would meet
to plan and pray for that morning's activities. On any given
Sunday morning, the pastor would simply materialize at
the gathering of children's workers or parking lot volunteers
or greeters. This allowed him to have quick, unscripted
conversations, take a moment or two to communicate vision,
and thank the people giving of their discretionary time and
energy. Especially during an effort to change the culture,
such small yet impactful moments are a key ingredient in the
secret sauce. The leader is a visible, incarnational presence—
not someone a long way away randomly hurling change
initiatives like thunderbolts from on high.

5. *Reward Risk Taking.* Because anxiety is high during a time
of culture change and formation, tolerance for risk is low.
This goes both ways. Leaders are anxious, knowing their
jobs could be on the line, so their tendency is to keep
their powder dry and make incremental, technical changes
only. Followers are caught up in the tension and anxiety of
uncertainty with so much changing around them, and so
they are inclined to keep their heads low and plod ahead.
Imagine Gage's team going through their culture change.
For years they had been rewarded for a *caliente* culture, built
around taste and spice and no heed for health. Now, the
company was saying it intended to become grounded in
healthy ingredients and a sustainable lifestyle. How do you
risk when your assumptions have been challenged? Wise
leaders know that part of the secret sauce is the ingredient
that says, "You can risk and experiment. We won't tolerate
such; we will encourage it. We will reward you for trying

new things and taking risks." Nothing lessens anxiety more than the sense that "I can try and fail and still have a place here." That goes for life and human relationships, as well as work, by the way.

6. *Resist Consensus Building.* Engage people in conversations, but not for the sake of consensus. Engage people in conversation so that you gather the most information possible to make great decisions. One of the management consultants Gage hired gave him advice like this: "Don't move ahead until you have gained the approval and agreement of everyone on the team." This is bad advice. Now, it is critical that a change leader build a guiding coalition of influential team members who can influence others. And, at the end of the day, it is better to have more people bought in than not. But we have learned through hard experience that when you are in the process of forging a healthy culture, not everyone will buy in. Some cannot deal with the anxiety of change. Others have a vested interest or key alliances rooted in the old culture. Others just will not get it. Others are simply oppositional by nature. Not everyone will buy in, at least not everyone will buy in right away. This is where the leader has a most challenging, yet invigorating balancing act. It is vitally important to engage people in the process of change. That is actually named in the very definition of secret sauce! But input, once a leader has made a directional decision, is not about approval. It is about helping the leader make good decisions with as much information as possible. Here, it is all about framing and expectations. There are both formal and informal structures for gaining input, but it has to be clear what the input is for. It is not a vote. It is a respectful asking for wisdom earned from experience that will help the leader be the best steward possible as the cultural change is implemented.

7. *Let Ideas Percolate.* Unless your industry is collapsing around you or your business is months away from foreclosure, time is on your side. Recognizing that a change in culture is necessary is much of the battle. But remember that your culture did not get to where it is overnight. And it will not change overnight. And remember that as a leader you see further ahead than followers do because your job is to see the big picture, standing on the balcony looking down over the dance floor. It took Gage ten years to succeed in creating a winning culture, only to find out that his next right leadership move was to disrupt the status quo and forget everything he had learned. The switch from a *caliente* company to promoting a healthy lifestyle will not come overnight, either. Incremental victories and progress matter. Do not let up, but do not be discouraged if at times the pace feels too slow to you.

8. *Raise the Temperature.* Expose competing values. Encourage conflict. We do not know if there is a more important leadership lesson than this one. The work of a leader is not to squelch but rather to spotlight competing values, especially around matters of belief and behavior. In a book Kevin coauthored with TAG colleague Ken Tucker, *The Leadership Triangle*, he pointed out that there are three types of challenges facing leaders: a) tactical—where the problem is relatively simple and what is required is expertise or an expert; b) strategic—where the problem is a change in the outside environment of the organization and the leader must marshal and synthesize the right facts and people; and c) transformational—where the problem involves competing values. Transformational leadership is where the real work of leadership is done. Real change cannot happen unless people are allowed to see where their values compete and where they differ, and where this is done in an environment of acceptance. Once these competing values are surfaced, the work is to

define, clarify, and hone the values all will share. Heifetz talks about "creating urgency," and this is what he means. A wise leader will look for critical points where she can say, "Look, we are not in alignment here—we have to look at why, even if it is uncomfortable and it hurts." Competing values often try to hide in dark corners. Bringing them out into the open casts light in and allows for everyone to be seeing the same thing.

9. *Give Grief Room.* Grief may strike you as an odd theme to end our very positive Ten Commandments toward a very positive thing—brewing a secret sauce that will create a wonderful and healthy organizational culture. But we have to face it down. When people lose something, they grieve. When things change—even for the better—there is loss. Loss of what is familiar, expected. Loss of a sense that "I know how to navigate this world." Perhaps loss of power or position or title. Let's stare this Tenth Commandment down at some length.

10. *Create the Quest.* Remember that these three things are at the heart of what it means to be human: to belong, to contribute, and to make a difference. And because this is true, these three things are at the heart of what it means to have a great culture. Make these three things—belong, contribute, make a difference—part of your scorecard, one of the metrics by which you judge the success of your organization. Be overt in telling your people, "I want these three things for you and I will leverage my influence to make sure you have opportunities to fulfill them." Think about the power of that—you are speaking to the deepest, truest, most universal aspirations of the human heart, something that is innate to everyone—and saying, "What is valuable to you is valuable to me and as a leader I want to create space for those things to happen for you in the course of your work life, your life as a volunteer." This is what creates the highest levels of engagement among people.

So why is the quest the secret sauce? Because it is where the real life change occurs. Scholars tell us that people are shaped most during times of emotional intensity. During our early years, these periods of emotional intensity are common as toddlers and adolescents. But in our adult years, these periods of emotional intensity are less frequent, but not less important. The secret sauce is all about how we handle people in the quest.

Change is not easy for anyone. Life is about transitions. It seems as though, at any given point, someone is either coming or going. These transitions can be inconsequential (someone leaving for work in the morning), or they can be life changing and even life shattering (death, war, social upheaval). Loss, and the anticipation of loss, brings with it an internal sense of anxiety.

Anxiety is the primary response to anticipated loss. We mentioned earlier in this chapter how a key ingredient in the secret sauce of culture change is helping others manage their anxiety. In the next chapter we will talk about how the leader can manage his own anxiety.

If anxiety is the response to anticipated loss, grief is the response to a loss that has actually occurred. Grief is a natural response to loss. It is the emotional suffering one feels when something or someone the individual loves is taken away. There is always real loss when there is a change in the culture of an organization. We cannot deny that or wish it away in the heat of battle or the busyness of forging a new culture. Again, it is part of what makes the quest itself the secret sauce.

People experience anxiety as they anticipate loss, anticipating the pain that grief will bring. When the grief comes, the pain is realized. Here is the deal—the pain must be honored. Not to honor it is to risk alienating your followers forever, or at least for a long time, because we are tapping into more than "workplace issues" here. We are tapping into the human heart. And this is precisely why incentive programs, compensation changes, goal setting, and other management techniques fail when it comes to creating culture.

If a person has a history of unresolved past losses, the current loss will intensify the experience of grief, reviving old fears, angers, hurts, depression. In turn, this will affect their morale, engagement, and ownership in their work life.

It is critical that leaders understand that this process exists—as part of the quest—and understand at least the rudiments of how it works. If you are forging change, people will be grieving, and part of the secret sauce is that you offer a healing ingredient that will help people move through their grief rather than helping them to avoid it.

The writer Eckhart Tolle tells the story of a woman he would visit who was riddled with cancer. She had months to live, and was facing death with increasing serenity. But, once, when he called, she was unusually distressed. A diamond ring of hers had gone missing, and she feared that her housekeeper might have stolen it.

Tolle asked her four simple questions about the way she was feeling, which helped her. Each question was followed by a pause. You might try to imagine what it is like to lose something *you* treasure, as she did.

Do you realize you will have to let go of it at some point, perhaps quite soon?

How much more time do you need before you will be willing to let it go?

Will you become less when you let go of it?

Has *who you are* been diminished by the loss?

As the woman grew more ill, she began to give most of her things away, including to the woman whom she thought might have stolen the ring. And she became filled with more and more joy. "'Now I understand something Jesus said that never made much sense to me before,' she said. 'If someone takes your shirt, let them have your coat as well.'"

A WALK OFF THE RANGE

After their discussion and brief practice session, Chip walked Gage to his rental car. "I hope you don't mind my using you as the inspiration for the Secret Sauce, my friend. As I mentioned, you have been a great catalyst for me in taking my own thinking on life and leadership to the next level. I am grateful to you. Don't worry, I'm not writing a book. I'm just trying to help the folks around here understand their own lives and sense of calling a little better. If I can do that, I'll feel like I've made a difference."

Gage was a little embarrassed. "Chip, I am honored in my own weird way, man. But before I get in this car and head back West, one thing is still gnawing at me..."

Chip said nothing, waiting patiently.

Gage gulped. "I mean, I hate to admit it, but I don't feel like I quite have it down. I mean, have down this total wrap-my-mind-around-it understanding of the Secret Sauce. Can you take one more run at if for this dumb cook?"

Chip laughed. "Gage, you are anything but dumb. It's simple, but it is the kind of simplicity that is the far side of complexity, not the near side. You have to go through the cauldron to get to it. And you have gone through the cauldron.

"Here, let me try to put it this way:

"The secret to creating a great culture is more about the quest than the end product. The quest is king. Or queen. Or prime minister, if you will!

"The quest is everything.

"Remember what I said before that I have learned over the years. All people have an inborn, innate desire to belong, to contribute, and to make a difference. A great culture draws on all of these universal human desires. But such a culture doesn't just happen. It has to be created through a process that involves all of those people as they realize the kind of life they were meant to live.

"The Secret Sauce, Gage, is the quest that you lead your people on to get to your brilliant future and the healthy, thriving culture you have always envisioned. But the secret sauce is more about how you lead your people. It's your own quest, your own journey. Gage, think about all of the issues that you have faced over the last several years. You've dealt with your personal

demons. You've dealt with great success and equally great failures. You've seen your company rise and fall.

"The secret sauce isn't any one thing. It's the whole recipe! It's not just the ingredients or the temperature of the oven. It's the process of putting all of those pieces together that is the secret sauce! You see, many people think that the secret sauce is a formula. It's not. It's what makes your own journey and your own company unique.

"There are no shortcuts. Remember the first time I asked you THE *question? You weren't ready for it. It took a couple of years. Being patient and trusting the process—that is the secret sauce, Gage.*

"It's time for you to cook up your own Secret Sauce and be a legend!

"See you soon, my friend."

Chip loaded the clubs into Gage's trunk. Gage closed his door and was soon winding down the mountain toward the airport.

As he drove he felt something building and welling inside of him. He sensed his most important moment as a chef and a leader was on his immediate horizon. Because now he was starting to understand the secret of the sauce.

9

IT REALLY IS ALL ABOUT YOU . . . SORT OF

TWO YEARS LATER

A lot had happened in the last 24 months. Gage had entered into "the quest" with gusto, stirring the secret sauce every day and engaging his people at every step. The already successful company had transformed both its marketing and manufacturing operations and had had stunning success with new lines of healthy and organic food.

After a lot of work, Gage and his team had managed to make their signature mole sauce much healthier and pretty much every bit as tasty. They had won industry awards, been honored by thought leaders in the sustainable movement like Mark Bittman of the New York Times, *and grown in profitability. Gage was now even in talks with Food Network executives about a new show devoted to tasty yet healthy meals.*

Life was good, but the now nearly middle-aged Gage was starting to feel a bit restless. He thought he knew why.

Chip had been out to Gage's offices once a year and had quickly been accepted as a trusted adviser and confidant. But as Gage looked back over the last 12 years he realized that his clearest times of thinking had come in the cool, thin mountain air of North Carolina. So, he flew into Charlotte and grabbed a rental car to head up to Granger Mountain. This time, he was bound and determined to play some golf, so the last thing he did before boarding the rental car shuttle was to grab his clubs from baggage claim.

It was midafternoon when Gage made it to the golf club. He had taken the red-eye, but he was energized. It was a midsummer day—hot and muggy at Charlotte Douglas International airport, but 20 degrees cooler and much less humid in the mountains.

As he had so many times before, Gage drove his rental car over the winding approach road to the club and parked in the lot. When he got out of his car, he paused for a minute to savor the mountain air and the breathtaking scenery.

"Moving a little slower these days, aren't you, old friend?"

Gage grinned and turned to see Chip waiting on him. They exchanged hugs.

"What, are you saying I am getting old, Chip?"

Chip held up his hands in mock defensiveness. "No, no, no! You are way younger than me! I just remember the first time you pulled into this parking lot, squealing the tires on that red hot rod, bounding out like some hyper puppy dog, looking to conquer the world and chew up the scenery. Now it actually looks like you have an appreciation for your surroundings!"

"You are right, my friend," Gage responded. "A lot has changed in 12 years, but I'm not sure my golf game has. I'm so bad I have to yell 'fore' even before I swing! One of these days I am going to hire a teaching professional who actually knows what he's doing!"

Chip laughed loud and long. "OK, OK, you win. How about this for an idea? I rarely get to play, but I had a cancellation for a late afternoon lesson. What about if you hang out for a while and we sneak in a quick nine as the sun is going down? Remember that 'million-dollar view' of the mountain on hole number eight? Wouldn't that be fun to play at twilight?"

A couple hours later Gage and Chip stood at the tee box for hole eight. Both hit fine tee shots on the par four, and Gage found himself 125 yards away with an uphill lie. The crowned green sloped sharply down to the fairway and was lined by a cool bubbling mountain stream on the left, with greenside bunkers on the other three sides. Gage breathed deeply, considered the yardage and the terrain, and chose his nine iron. The pitching wedge was his go-to club for 125 yards, but this lie meant he would need more carry. The green was so high above him that he couldn't even see the flag.

He smiled to himself as he recalled that back in his early days of playing golf he would have been likely to have chosen less club than he actually needed and to utter some inanity like "grip it and rip it!" before a wild swing that would land him in the water.

Today, he chose the nine iron, and stood behind the ball, visualizing his shot. He stepped up and took one smooth and slow practice swing. Then he addressed the ball and executed a smooth backswing, a powerful downswing, and finished with his body turned toward the flag, at least where he thought it was.

The ball soared through the air, bounced off the hill behind the green and rolled back to within six feet of the cup.

Trying to hide his self-satisfied grin, Gage fixed his divot and looked up to see Chip not addressing his own ball but smiling at him.

"What?" Gage asked.

"It's just that I am amazed at the golfer you are becoming, Gage," said Chip.

Gage said nothing. He wasn't sure he could.

As they strode toward the green, Chip turned his head toward Gage.

"Hey, I get the feeling you want to talk about something. Am I right?"

"You know how well we have done over the last few years. I owe most if not all of that to you."

Chip held up a hand in protest, but Gage waved him away.

"No, I am serious. I had to execute the strategy and surrender to the quest. I expected golf lessons. Then you started giving me business lessons. But the journey has really been personal for me. You have been my guiding mentor. Don't think I don't know that.

"Anyway, I am getting close to this whole dumb middle-aged thing, and I am starting to think about the future. Well, not the future so much. I am pretty sure we can keep the business on the rails. Think of all the tools I have because of you. But I am thinking. And . . . OK, this is a little embarrassing. But I am thinking about my legacy."

Chip said nothing, just kept walking. They arrived at the edge of the green. There was no one else on the course, so they were not in a hurry.

Chip reached into his golf bag and took out a bottle of water. Turning toward the mountain vista, he took a long drink before capping the bottle, returning it to the bag, and turning back to Gage.

"I figured you might be, sooner rather than later," he said softly. "What does that look like for you?"

Gage breathed deeply. "OK, can we stop and talk?"

Chip glanced back to make sure nobody else was approaching the green, then nodded.

"Do you know this guy named Jim Noble, down in Charlotte?" Gage asked.

"I have heard of him," Chip responded. "I met a guy from my men's group for lunch one day at his restaurant—'Roosters,' I think, near South-Park Mall."

"Yeah, that's the guy. So, he is not a huge deal on the national scene in terms of the celebrity stuff, but all the guys in the industry know and respect him. He has some awesome restaurants. But what is really grabbing my attention is this charity stuff he's doing.

"Chip, in uptown Charlotte he has this whole restaurant—I mean a really, really good restaurant—called The King's Kitchen. Check this out—100 percent of the proceeds from the restaurant go to feed the poor in Charlotte, the region, and the world. That's the kind of thing that has never been on my radar. But can you imagine what kind of impact he is having?

"Even more, this particular restaurant hires people other people won't hire—people just out of prison. Guys who are addicts. People who couldn't get a job at Taco Bell because of their rap sheets or personal struggles with drugs or alcohol, who get to work at a great restaurant under a master chef and have that on their resumes.

"I mean, who does that?"

Gage pulled his iPhone out of his bag and texted Chip the website, www.chefjimnoble.com.

"You can read more about this guy there. He does it he says out of his love for God. For me, I am still trying to figure out who God is, but the point is that he is doing something with his success. And it is making

something inside of me get excited. I want to do that too. We've made a lot of strides in terms of talking about sustainability and healthy lifestyles and helping kids eat right and exercise while still enjoying tasty food, but I have this feeling there is more for me. For us.

"Does that make any sense?"

Chip gazed up at the mountains again.

"Gage, you are talking legacy now. There is simply nothing more important you could be talking about. I personally think this is the essence of what we're created to be.

"Early on, you had to learn how to manage an enterprise. Then you had to learn how to manage people. Then you had to learn how to disruptively manage in such a way that you called the status quo into question. Then you learned about the secret sauce, and how the quest itself leads to cultural change.

"And now, you are about to learn the most important management lesson of all.

"Gage, let's putt out before it gets dark."

Gage felt like a kid who had just had Christmas morning deferred so that his parents could sip coffee and read the morning newspaper, but he went along, completing his birdie with a delicate sidehill putt.

The shadows were long now and so the two friends headed for the clubhouse. When they got within 50 yards, Gage couldn't stand it any longer.

"Chip, what's the most important management lesson of all? Come on, man!"

Chip walked a few more yards without speaking. Then he stopped and faced Gage.

"Gage, my friend, I believe we are all created with a desire to belong, to contribute, and make a difference. You've been through a lot of that with your company. You've created a culture that has allowed those things to happen. But the most important management lesson of all is how to do this for you.

"It is the process of becoming that counts more than what you've become. I heard a great quote recently. The guy said, 'This life therefore is

not health, but healing, not being but becoming, not rest but exercise. We are not yet what we shall be, but we are growing toward it, the process is not yet finished, but it is going on, this is not the end, but it is the road.'

 "The process itself is where it's at. The process of learning to belong, figuring out how to contribute, and ultimately, your own journey of making a difference. Gage, the secret sauce isn't the end result, it's the road that leads there. That's your legacy, Gage."

MANAGING SELF

As we have mentioned, the genesis of our book was our TED (The Engagement Dashboard) study, which has looked at hundreds of organizations of all types over 15 years.

 Our goal has been to poke under the hood of high-capacity organizations, finding out what made them work, what was scalable, and how their quests could inform the quest of other organizations anywhere.

 There has simply been no organization that excelled more on TED than one of our clients, Forney Construction, led by Tom Forney, based in Houston.

 He has done well, no doubt. His previous construction firm that he started with some college friends was sold to the giant Balfour Beatty. His current company, Forney Construction, scored the highest on TED of any company we have ever surveyed. It is a success story like few we have experienced.

 One obvious arena of success for them has been Citizenship, a component of culture that we discussed earlier. Their core values form an acronym, SERVICE. Far from being cheesy, these values pack a real punch:

 Serve God, others, then self.
 Embrace challenges.
 Respect others.
 Volunteerism
 Integrity

Commitment

Empower people.

We could easily have made Forney Construction our marquee example in our section on citizenship. After all, they provide 24 PAID hours a year to each employee to volunteer in a not-for-profit of their choice, and they offer matching gifts to employees of up to $300 for not-for-profit contributions. In addition, one-third of the company's annual net profit is returned to the community through in-kind and cash contributions. They have never fallen short of this commitment. They are stellar in this regard.

But we chose to include Forney in this last chapter because they excel at the most perhaps the most important TED evaluation of all. Dependability. This dimension is the only dimension in the entire survey that requires only one sentence to sum it up: *Management can be counted upon to come through when needed.* It is tough to overemphasize the importance of this metric. It is all important and determinative.

People will put up with almost any "what" if they get the "why"—we are engaged in something great and life altering and useful and good, and we can count on our leaders.

This single question – "Can I count on my leaders?" – was the only other question to correlate to every other question in TED. In a very real sense the quest for dependability is where the recipe for the Secret Sauce resides.

And here is the secret about this. It is all about the leader. What we mean by that is that for the quest to be pure, unencumbered, successful, the leader must get out of the way. The leader matters less than the cause.

You have to get "self" out of the way. Lao-Tzu once said that "a leader is best when people barely know that he exists."

Can you as a leader be counted on to come through, for others, no matter what? Will you get your hands dirty, will you walk out the talk of the values, will you incarnate the code, will you risk losing yourself to disrupt the status quo?

Can you be depended on to come through when needed? And, if you are in the early stages of your career, are you putting in place the factors to develop the kind of character where you will be depended upon at the end of the day?

Are you getting yourself out of the way?

TOM FORNEY'S STORY

"In five years and four months, we went from 'we can't afford a fax machine' to 50 million dollars in revenue. We did this after starting one month before the worst economic depression this country has experienced in 69 years," Tom Forney told us.

Tom's is a Sun Belt success story, an up-by-your-bootstraps start-up grinding along to become one of the most successful commercial construction firms in the United States.

Along the way, Tom sold his first company to pursue personal passions.

Guatemala had his heart, and so Tom invested significant personal resources in health care and education for the people there, at one point walking away from riches to leverage everything on a not-for-profit venture to love Guatemalans. Following this experience, Tom and his wife, Holly, donated 60 percent of their personal net worth to found a nonprofit start-up in the form of a camp for children with special needs, Camp Aranzazu, located in Rockport, Texas.

This took him to new levels of Service, but he could never get away from the thing that made him HIM—forging a company that did exceptional construction work for entities ranging from huge hospitals to local churches—all with a bent toward excellence, beauty, and functionality.

Forney has had a fascinating sort of back-and-forth career—going from highly profitable companies to risk-it-all-on-a-vision nonprofits. His success in the construction world speaks for itself—both in terms of profits, esteem, and employee engagement. Again, no company has ever done better on the TED.

But his comments about nonprofit leadership are equally fascinating.

We asked him what were his secrets to successful leadership of those organizations.

He mentioned two things.

"First, you have to be accountable for absolutely every dollar. Really, this is the case in for profits as well, but when you are basing your revenues on the contributions of donors, you have to account for every penny."

Then, Forney made an interesting pivot in the conversation.

"I have brought this understanding over to the construction business as well, which is for-profit. We need a purpose beyond being a general contractor. We're not doing this to be the best, fastest, most unique builder . . . it's about providing service to our customers just like a nonprofit services its constituents. We don't compete on price as much as service. We want clients, not one-time customers . . . our clients have stayed with us and we grew with them as they grew."

This is a very big deal. Tom Forney is talking about bringing the ethos of the nonprofit—the very nature of the nonprofit quest—into the highly competitive world of general contracting on a grand scale. It is all about mission, credibility, dependability.

It is this passion, played out in the day-to-day quest, pressed into the mundaneness of policies and procedures, that results in the over-the-top scores on the The Engagement Dashboard we saw.

This is the Secret Sauce of Forney Construction.

We had a fascinating conversation with Tom that ranged over a couple of hours, and he said an awful lot of things worth noting. But there was one story that stood out.

His company was spearheading a major renovation for a high-end country club. The deadline was fierce, and the challenges were awesome.

At one point they had to complete the renovation of the "bag room," the place where the members stored and kept their golf clubs.

Although Tom did not know it at the time, the pressure to finish on time and with minimal disruption was extremely important to the club. The following week Tom got this e-mail from his contact at the club:

> *Tom,*
>
> *Just wanted to let you know that Terry Elder and his crew hit a homerun for us on Monday. We had pulled all of our bags out and put them into the pro shop…preparing for the 3 week period to build the new bag room. I went to bed Sunday night feeling like I had bitten off much more than I could chew…it was going to be a HARD 3 weeks because of how crowded we were.*
>
> *When I got in on Tuesday, my staff told me how Terry and his crew had come up with the idea of cutting the old bag racks in half and using them to help us take more advantage of our space.*
>
> *I really appreciate the fact that Terry didn't have to do that, (remember I had said multiple times that we were ok) but he could tell the issues we were about to face and solved our problem before they happened.*
>
> *Sincere thanks and thought you should know his efforts!!!!*
>
> *Gary*

One of Tom's team members had developed—in the crush of pressure—an elegant and resourceful solution to a seemingly insoluble problem. The results? A satisfied customer, and a highly energized and engaged team member. Terry knew he did not need permission to spend the money and time. He never even notified Tom of the problem. Terry knew the core values gave him the empowerment to Service the client the same way he knew Tom would. There was no need to ask for guidance.

What became clear as we talked with Tom was that the key to this radical top-to-bottom success was not a strategy or even a vision. It was a total congruence between the leader and his enterprise. Tom Forney has figured out himself and who he is as a leader. His conversation is laced with self-awareness and wisdom. He knows who he is, and this profound sense of "self" filters down to every level of his organization. This is the final whisk, the crowning ingredient of the Secret Sauce—the leader who understands and leads himself or herself.

What does self-leadership require? Four things, we believe.

KNOW YOUR STRENGTHS

Great leadership is not rooted in fixing your weaknesses. Goodness knows we all have enough of those. But greatness does not come through addressing them.

Any competent golf professional will help his student build upon his strengths rather than try to fix his weaknesses. A student who is 5'5" and 120 lbs. is not likely to crush the ball 280 yards off of the tee. She is more likely to be adept at the short game, with touch around the green and in the short game. The pro will start there.

An introvert is not likely to be a smooth pitchman. But he may well have a unique ability to read body language and unspoken cues.

Go with what you have. If you are logical and given to process, major in that. If you love people and motivating others, make this your focus. Know yourself.

Our colleagues Ken Tucker, Shane Roberson, and Todd Hahn make a case for this in their book *Your Intentional Difference: One Word Changes Everything*.

Here is their basic premise.

Eighty-five percent of what we do, most people can do.

Ten percent of what we do, select others can be trained and developed to do.

But there is a unique 5 percent that you and only you can do the way you do it. It is your uniqueness, lived large.

You were made different to make a difference, and this difference is an expression of your Intentional Difference.

Whether or not you use the Intentional Difference process or not, it is vital that you know your strengths and that you do everything you can to maximize them. Perhaps you will use the DISC inventory or the Meyers-Briggs or the Clifton StrengthsFinder assessments. Perhaps you will survey trusted confidants who have seen you in good moments and challenging ones.

Whatever tack you take, you will want to make sure that you know your strengths, who you are, what you are made to do, and that you organize your life around these endeavors.

MANAGE YOUR RED ZONE

One of the "stickiest" concepts in our consulting practice is the idea of Red Zone/Blue Zone when it comes to conflict resolution. Jim in particular has done a lot of work in this area, and he wrote *Thriving through Ministry Conflict* with Joseph Jurkowski and Todd Hahn to flesh it out.

Wherever we go, whatever kind of organization we are working with, we continue to hear that the simple concepts of Red Zone/Blue Zone pay life- and career-changing dividends.

Here's the deal: conflict must be embraced, not shunned. As a matter of fact, resistance can be our ally, not our enemy.

It works like this. Every time we face a conflict of any kind, we can choose to respond from the Red Zone or the Blue Zone. The Red Zone is where we personalize conflict. The Blue Zone is where we focus the conflict around competing values.

When personal values intrude into organizational conflict, we end up talking past one another. But when we keep the conflict focused on values and interests that transcend the personal, we have the chance to actually thrive through the conflict because it heightens trust and leads to a clearer vision of our values and goals.

Check out this chart, designed to help you navigate the differences between Red Zone and Blue Zone behaviors:

Blue Zone	Red Zone
This conflict is professional	This conflict is personal
It is about the organization	It is about me, and you
The mission of the organization rules	Emotions rule without being acknowledged
I must protect the team and the org	I must protect myself
The conflict is about discussing values	The conflict escalates to destructive levels

Where does our Red Zone behavior come from?

Two places: our pain and our view of the world. Left unacknowledged, these two forces can consign us to a life of living in the Red Zone.

If you have stuck with us this far, we consider you to be a friend. And, as our friend, we do not want for you to live in Red Zone when it comes to conflict. Living in the Red Zone can derail careers, hamstring personal relationships, even destroy organizations.

It is vital that we learn to face pushback and resistance from the Blue Zone, not the Red Zone.

Here are four principles that will help you see resistance as your ally, not your enemy:

1. Maintain clear focus—one eye on the moment, the other on the big picture.
2. Embrace resistance. Move toward, not away from the sources of resistance. This is hard, because our tendency is to defeat, run around, or deny resistance. It is a learned behavior, so be patient with yourself! Resistance is your ally because it shows you that your current strategies are not fully working, and it gives you options to move ahead.
3. Respect those who resist, by monitoring your emotions, avoiding the Red Zone, and always telling the truth.

4. Join with the resistance. Look for common themes, values, and patterns, looking together for ways the situation needs to change.

There is one core concept when it comes to conflict that we have found simultaneously hard to accept and liberating.

YOU ARE PART OF THE PROBLEM

This is hard for us to understand! We think others are the problem—they are obstacles, or opponents, or deadwood, even if well intentioned. But a key component of self-management is understanding that in any conflict I bring stuff to the table too.

We love to say "The problem is you . . . so know yourself."

Here is why that works.

I cannot change you—at least in the long run. But I can change me. And if I can change me, I can change the dynamic that has us in opposition. At the very least, if I change me, I open up more options for both of us. And when I focus on changing me, the problem itself has this strange tendency to recede and be put into perspective.

At TAG we have a framework we call the 3-D Method for navigating conflict. Try this out the next time you face resistance!

DIALOGUE

Encourage people to simply state personal opinions without feedback or interruption from others. Each person shares an opinion and that opinion is not judged.

DISCUSSION

Now, days or weeks later, people can agree or disagree with each other. No decisions are made at this point, but points of view are aired. The discussion phase allows you to reveal competing values, so everyone can see the issues that are really in play.

DECISION

At the decision point, conflict will emerge to be sure, but it will be much less significant because the group has already processed the issue through dialogue and discussion.

If you are the leader of the group, this is where you earn your pay—it may be time to make a hard decision if consensus does not emerge!

BE DEPENDABLE

In a sense, this is the true heart of the matter. In modern-day organizational life, people expect many things from their leaders, but dependability is not a word that is high on their list. People expect power plays, unreasonable expectations, skillful politics, and my-career-first sorts of attitudes. But not dependability.

And that is precisely why dependability is so important.

Bottom line, when a leader is dependent, it creates a sense of safety in her followers. And safety is something that is in short supply in our culture and in our workplaces.

This is not a "soft skill." People who feel unsafe add in self-protecting ways, which shuts out collaboration and are often dishonest. It is understandable—when your emotional and financial well-being may be on the line, you are going to protect yourself.

But when people feel safe, they are free to give and free to risk and free to innovate.

One of our client companies is committed to safety for its people. Not just workplace safety but emotional safety.

Over the last few years, a number of its employees have endured personal hardship. In some other companies, in several cases, these employees might have been candidates for dismissal. In many organizations, they might have been escorted to the door by security.

But this company values people to such a great degree that it is willing to come alongside them and support them during difficult times, offering reduced workloads for temporary periods, counseling support, and patience. This benefits the employees involved greatly but other, non-affected employees see it as well. The message: you can depend on us.

This is not to say that there is an endless reserve of patience and that production and the bottom line do not matter. But the organization is more than a machine—it is a community.

Dependability involves leaders coming through on their commitments, honoring the values the organization claims, treating people with both individuality and equity, and genuinely caring for employees as people who have families, lives, interests, and needs that are outside the scope of the organization.

When people feel safe, they can venture beyond themselves. This is what allows them to belong, contribute, and make a real and lasting difference.

THE GRAND FINALE?

As hard as it was for them to believe, today was the first day Chip and Gage had ever met outside of the mountains of North Carolina and the environs of the golf club.

Tonight, they were attending a very special event in the borough of Brooklyn in New York City. Not far from former president Bill Clinton's offices, in an area that for years had been depressed and crime ridden, Gage was opening a new restaurant. And Chip was his honored guest.

The atmosphere was beautiful, imbued with Gage's signatures— warmth, bright colors, delectable aromas, and a sense of genuine and true hospitality.

Gage rose to give a toast.

"Many people are responsible for getting us to this night. My mother, first, who instilled in me a love of cooking, food, and sauces. I can still smell the aroma wafting from her kitchen! She also taught me about passion and values. Not to mention the restaurant business!

"My incredible team, which has stood behind me in good times and bad, when I knew what I was doing and when I had no clue.

"But I want to pay very special tribute tonight to one very special friend, Chip Long, who has been my mentor and guide for a long time now."

He pointed Chip out but, predictably, his friend ducked his head and went a bit red faced with embarrassment.

"Several years ago, I began a journey of battling my own demons. I avoided the deeper questions of life. I masked my pain with alcohol. I've been sober for four years, eight months, and three days. Chip helped me find my way. The beauty of this restaurant," Gage continued, "is that the people who work here are all people who have struggled with some form of addiction, like I have. Some have been in prison, some have been on the streets, but tonight we are all in Caliente.

"And that is what we are about in this company. Joy, food, community, second and third chances. And, most of all, great sauce!"

Gage raised his champagne flute in the air and enjoined the crowd: "To my friend Chip, to our secret sauce, and to this grand finale for my career!"

The crowd erupted in applause and began to swell toward Gage, patting him on the back, pumping his hand, congratulating him.

A few minutes later, Gage returned to his table, where he was seated next to Chip.

"So what did you think, my friend?"

Chip's smile was broad and his eyes twinkled.

"You did a great job and this is a great job. But this is no grand finale."

Gage looked puzzled.

"What do you mean?" he asked.

Chip put his hand on his friend's shoulder.

"Because now that you have discovered the Secret Sauce, there is no finale. There is only beginning."

NOTES

1 HOLY MOLE

1. Shawn Parr, "Culture Eats Strategy for Lunch," FAST COMPANY, January 24, 2012; http://www.fastcompany.com/1810674/culture-eats-strategy-lunch).
2. Jason Snell, "Steve Jobs: Making a Dent in the Universe," *Macworld*, October 6, 2011; http://www.macworld.com/article/1162827/steve_jobs_making_a_dent_in_the_universe.html.

2 A *CALIENTE* COMPANY

1. Peter Drucker, *The Essential Drucker*, Collins Business Essentials, 2001, iv.

3 IT'S HOT IN HERE!

1. Karen Mulady, "Fair-trade Coffees Finding Favor among Small Retailers," *Seattle Post-Intelligencer*, November 21, 2001; http://www.seattlepi.com/business/article/Fair-trade-coffees-finding-favor-among-small-1072462.php.

4 IF I'M THE PROBLEM, THEN WHAT?

1. Alex Gibney, director, *The Smartest Guys in the Room*, Jigsaw Productions, DVD, 2005.

2. Tony Simons, *The Integrity Dividend*, Jossey-Bass, 2008.

3. http://www.greatplacetowork.com/best-companies/100-best-companies-to-work-for

6   WHEN YOU'VE LOST YOUR SAUCE

1. See Charles Handy, *The Age of Paradox*, Harvard Business Press, 1995, for a helpful discussion.

7   LETTING IT ALL GO

1. http://www.canadianbusiness.com/blogs-and-comment/stop-using-gretzky-where-the-puck-is-quote/

8   WHAT'S THE SECRET SAUCE?

1. Ronald Heifetz and Marty Linsky, excerpt from *Leadership on the Line: Staying Alive through the Dangers of Leading*, May 28, 2002, hbs.edu; http://hbswk.hbs.edu/archive/2952.html.

INDEX

3-D Method for navigating conflict, 182

AcadeMIX, 152
Academy of Management, 132
accountability, 29, 47, 66, 96, 142, 177
actions, 96–7
AIG, 134
American Apparel, 73, 96
anxiety
    change and, 159, 162
    managing, 156–7
    reframing and, 113, 117
    risk and, 158–9
Apple, 16, 97–8
appropriate risk, 70–1
atmosphere, 44–5
attracting top talent, 27, 30–1, 142
Auburn University, 138–42

Bank of America, 134
Beane, Billy, 32
Being Mortal (Gawande), 119
Blockbuster, 133
Bolsinger, Tod, 107, 112, 114, 119, 121
brands, 97–100
Bush, Lori, 89

Canoeing the Mountains (Bolsinger), 112, 121
Cardiovascular Group of Northern Virginia, 95
change, dealing with, 132–8
    consumer appetites, 133–4
    demographics, 133
    economics, 134
    leadership and, 136–8

media, 134
    regulations, 133
    technology, 133
"Chaplinesque," 135
Charney, Dov, 73, 96
Chase Memorial Nursing Home, 120
cheating, 74, 106
Chick-fil-A, 16
Clifton StrengthsFinder, 31, 91, 180
Coach K
    see Krzyzewski, Mike
code, 16–17, 86–90, 94, 154, 175
collegiality, 28–9
common language, creating, 32–3
communication, 66–9
competing values, exposing, 160–1
competitors, 138
conflict, 131, 156, 160, 180–2
connection, 15
consensus building, resisting, 159
consistency, 64–5
consumer appetites, changes in, 133–4
Cooking Channel, 7
core ideology, 86–91
Costco, 10–11
Countryside, 134
Create Good Foundation, 49–50
    see also Pura Vida
credibility, 47
culture
    benefits of, 12–14
    building healthy culture, 10–17
    code, 87–8
    core ideology, 86–91
    defined, 12
    diagram, 86

culture—*Continued*
  fundamentals of, 85–91
  leadership and, 10, 18, 153–65
  strategy and, 12, 17, 49, 94, 153–4
  TAG's definition of, 17–18
  values and, 46

decisions, 87
demographics, changes in, 133
dependability, 63–6, 183–4
dialogue, 182
directing intentional conversations, 156
DISC profile, 31, 91, 180
disruptions
  external, 132–8
  internal, 138–43
Drucker, Peter, 30
Duke University, 63
Dye, Pat, 139

economics, changes in, 134
employees
  collegiality, 28–9
  empowerment, 27–8
  engagement, 31–4
  reliable management, 30–1
empowerment, 27–8
engagement, 31–4
Enron, 58, 60–1
external disruptions, 132–8

Fabre, Gage, 5–9, 21–6, 37–40, 55–7,
    81–5, 103–7, 114, 117, 119, 121,
    125–9, 147–51, 158–60, 163–5,
    169–74, 184–5
Facebook, 16
Fastow, Andrew, 58
feedback, 28, 30–1, 56, 138, 148, 182
Fields, Kathy, 88
Fifth Discipline, The (Senge), 130
Five Guys, 11
focus, 12–13
Food Network, 7–8, 81, 169
Forney, Tom, 174–9

Gawande, Atul, 119–20
Goldfish crackers, 99
Google, 41, 155
Granger Mountain Country Club,
    8, 21–3
Great Place to Work Institute, 63

grief, 161
Grove, Andy, 132

Hahn, Todd, 91, 179–80
Harley-Davidson, 97–9
Heifetz, Ronald, 130–1, 155, 161
heroes, 87
hiring, 46
Holy Mole, 7–8, 23–4
honesty, 63–4
honor, 47
Hussey, Jeff, 48–50

ideas, developing, 160
identity, 16
incentive systems, 33–4
infrastructure
  how, 93–4
  who, 91–3
initiative, 71–2
integrity, 73–5
Integrity Dividend, The (Simons), 62
Intel, 132
Intentional Difference process, 179–80
  see also *Your Intentional Difference*
intentionality, 33–4, 46, 65, 68–9, 94,
    96–7
interdependence, 42–4
internal disruptions, 138–43
interpretations, 115–17
intuition, 137

Jefferson, Thomas, 121
Jobs, Steve, 16
Johnson and Wales University, 103
Jones, Cullen, 140
Jurkowski, Joseph, 180

Krzyzewski, Mike, 63

Lay, Ken, 58, 61
leadership
  accountability and, 96
  change and, 135–8, 141–2
  collaboration and, 141
  communication and, 67–9
  culture and, 10, 18, 153–65
  decisions and, 87
  dependability and, 64–6, 183–4
  engagement and, 31–4
  identifying talent, 91–2